A 10-DAY ITINERARY IN THE HEART OF ITALY

Rome, Florence, Tuscany, Amalfi Coast
La Dolce Vita, History, Wine and Amalfi!

Isabella Di Marco

HOW TO GET AROUND IN ITALY   8
    TRAVELING BY TRAIN   10
    CAR RENTAL   14
    BY PLANE   17

DAY 1 AND 2 AND 3   20

ROMA   20

TRANSPORTATION   20
    FROM AND TO THE FIUMICINO INTERNATIONAL AIRPORT   20
    HANDY TIPS & SUGGESTIONS   21
        ELECTRIC SCOOTERS THE FUTURE IS HERE!   21
        ROMA BIKE SHARING   22

UNDERSTANDING THE FOUNDATION OF ROME   23
    THE SEVEN HILLS   23
    ANCIENT ROME'S MYTHOLOGY   24
    HISTORY OF THE ROMAN EMPIRE   25

DAY 1   ANCIENT ROME   27
    COLOSSEUM   28
    IL PALATINO - PALATINE HILL   30
    ROMAN FORUM   31
    RIONE MONTI   32
    PIAZZA VENEZIA E CAMPIDOGLIO   33
    TREVI FOUNTAIN   34
    PIAZZA DI SPAGNA – SPANISH STEPS   36
    DINNER OPTIONS   37

DAY 2   VATICAN CITY   38
    BASILICA DI SAN PIETRO   38
    MUSEI VATICANI E CAPPELLA SISTINA   40
    CASTEL SANT'ANGELO   42
    PIAZZA NAVONA   43

THE PANTHEON	44
CAMPO DÈ FIORI and GHETTO	45
L'ISOLA TIBERINA	46
AN EVENING IN TRASTEVERE	48

DAY 3 TESTACCIO, VILLA BORGHESE, CIRCO MASSIMO 51

VILLA BORGHESE	52
PINCIO AND PIAZZA DEL POPOLO	53
GALLERIA BORGHESE	54
AVENTINE AND CIRCUS MAXIMUS	54

DAY 4 AND 5 56

FIRENZE 56

A BIT OF INTRODUCTION	57
THE HISTORY MEDICI AND PAZZI FAMILIES	58
NAVIGATING FLORENCE	59
THE FLORENCE PASS	59
ACCOMMODATION	61

DAY 4 63

BASILICA DI SANTA MARIA NOVELLA	63
GALLERIA DELL'ACCADEMIA	63
DUOMO – GIOTTO'S TOWER – BATTISTERO	64
FOOD	68

DAY 5 70

PIAZZA DELLA SIGNORIA	70
GALLERIA DEGLI UFFIZZI	73
PONTE VECCHIO	73

DAY 6 75

TOSCANA 75

CHIANTI - SIENA	77

SAN GIMIGNANO	80
SIENA	82
AGRITURISMO	87

DAY 7 — 90

VAL D'ORCIA — 90

MONTEPULCIANO & MONTALCINO	92
SAN QUIRICO D'ORCIA	93
CHAPEL OF MADONNA DI VITALETA	94
PIENZA	95
AGRITURISMO	96

DAY 8 – 9 AND 10 — 98

AMALFI COAST — 98

Transportation what to know	98
Reaching The Amalfi Coast Transportation	99
From Naples to Positano	101
From Salerno to Positano	101
Recommended Transportation Websites	101
Welcome to the Amalfi Coast!	102
Where to Stay on the Amalfi Coast	103
Costs	104

POSITANO — 105

AMALFI — 106

SORRENTO — 108

PRAIANO — 109

IL SENTIERO DEGLI DEI (FROM AGEROLA TO NOCELLE)	110

RAVELLO — 111

CAPRI	**112**
DINING	**116**
GOING BACK TO ROMA AIRPORT	**118**
IN CASE OF EMERGENCY	**119**
A HEARTFELT THANK YOU AND A SPECIAL GIFT JUST FOR YOU	**120**

A 10-DAY ITINERARY THROUGH ITALY'S CULTURAL CAPITALS & MEDITERRANEAN WONDERS

FROM COLOSSEUMS TO CHIANTI CENTER AND CLIFFSIDE PARADISES

Ciao, traveler!
Welcome to your 10-day escape through some of Italy's most iconic and enchanting destinations!

Imagine waking up to the smell of espresso wafting through cobbled streets one day and the fresh sea breeze the next—this journey gives you the best of both worlds. Ten days are just enough to keep the itinerary lively yet leisurely, balancing both awe-inspiring sightseeing and those cherished **"dolce far niente"** moments.
The adventure kicks off in the eternal city of **Rome**, a sprawling urban museum where every corner whispers secrets of an ancient empire. Rome isn't just about gladiators and togas, though; it's a buzzing metropolis offering something for every type of explorer, whether you're an art junkie, a history buff, or a foodie (or hey, all three!).
During our three days in Rome, you'll have the opportunity to marvel at architectural wonders like the Colosseum and St. Peter's Basilica. But why stop at the classic guidebook recommendations? We'll dive into the lesser-known neighborhoods, perhaps discovering a charming osteria tucked away in a **Trastevere** alley or stumbling upon a contemporary art show in **Testaccio**.

Next, we take a scenic train ride through the rolling **hills of Tuscany to reach the Renaissance city of Florence**. Ah,

Florence—where art and life are celebrated with equal passion! Two days here will be followed by a vineyard-hopping spree through the picturesque **Tuscan countryside**.

We'll roam the medieval streets of **San Gimignano**, sip the famed **Brunello wines of Montalcino**, and squeeze in a detour to the historic towns of **Siena and Lucca**.

And let's not forget, we **wrap up this trip on the dramatic cliffs of the Amalfi Coast**. Get ready for three sun-soaked days in the coastal wonders of **Positano, Amalfi**, and perhaps a day trip to the stylish island of **Capri**. We'll guide you through every breathtaking hike, hidden beach, and romantic dinner spot this paradise has to offer.

But what makes this book truly unique are our curated experiences, insider tips, and detailed transportation guides. We're pulling back the curtain to reveal the authentic Italy, far beyond the tourist traps and cliche souvenirs.
So grab that suitcase and those sunglasses because an unforgettable Italian adventure full of culture, relaxation, and mouthwatering meals awaits you.

All aboard? Andiamo!

* In this guide, you'll find several QR codes **to enhance your exploration**.

HOW TO GET AROUND IN ITALY

Italy is a country that offers an abundance of things to see and do. With its rich culture, stunning landscapes, and world-renowned cuisine, it's no surprise that Italy is a popular destination for travelers from all over the world. But with so many options for transportation and places to visit, it can be hard to know where to start.
We'll be exploring the best ways to travel through Italy. From high-speed trains to local buses, we'll cover the pros and cons of each mode of transportation and provide tips for making the most of your journey.

Italy has a well-developed transportation network, so there are several options for traveling within the country. Here are some of the best ways to travel in Italy:

1. **Train**: Trains are one of the most popular way to travel in Italy, with a comprehensive network of regional, intercity, and high-speed trains that connect major cities and smaller towns. The high-speed trains, such as the Frecciarossa, Frecciargento, and Italo, are fast and efficient, while the regional and intercity trains are more affordable and often more convenient for shorter journeys.
2. **Bus**: Buses are another option for traveling in Italy, with a network of local, regional, and intercity buses that connect cities and towns across the country. Bus travel can be more affordable than train travel, but it's often slower and less comfortable.

3. **Car**: Renting a car is a good option for exploring Italy's countryside and smaller towns, where public transportation may be less frequent. However, driving in Italy can be challenging, especially in big cities, due to narrow roads, heavy traffic, and limited parking.
In Italy, *the majority of cars and scooters use manual shift transmission,* as opposed to automatic transmission. This means that drivers must be comfortable operating a clutch and shifting gears in order to drive in Italy. While automatic transmission vehicles are available for rent in some places, they may be less common or more expensive than manual shift vehicles. It's essential to check with your rental car company to see what transmission type is available and choose the option that best suits your driving experience and preferences.
4. **Scooter**: Renting a scooter is a fun and convenient way to explore Italy's cities and towns, especially in areas where car traffic and parking are challenging. Many cities, such as Rome and Florence, have a long tradition of scooter use, and rental shops can be found throughout the country. Scooters are affordable to rent and easy to park, and they provide a unique and authentic Italian travel experience. However, it's important to be aware of local traffic rules and safety guidelines, as driving a scooter can be more dangerous than other modes of transportation.
5. **Air**: Domestic air travel is available in Italy, with several airlines offering flights between major cities. However, flying is often more expensive than taking the train or bus, and it can be less convenient due to airport location and security procedures.

While it's true that driving in Italy can be a fun and unique experience, it's also important to note that Italian drivers are known for their sometimes aggressive and unpredictable behavior on the road. Drivers in big cities like Rome, Florence, and Milan can be particularly impatient and quick to honk their horns or cut in front of other vehicles. As a result, it's important for visitors to be alert and cautious when driving or using a scooter in Italy and to familiarize themselves with local traffic rules and customs to ensure a safe and enjoyable trip.

Overall, the best way to travel in Italy is by train. They are a great option for long-distance travel between major cities. Buses can be more affordable for shorter journeys but are often trapped in traffic on the main highways. Renting a car or a scooter is ideal for exploring the countryside and smaller towns while flying is a good option for longer distances or time-sensitive trips.

TRAVELING BY TRAIN

If you're looking to travel all over Italy, the train is an excellent option. Rome and Milan are the major transportation hubs in Italy, and it's served by both national and regional trains.

One of the most popular options is the high-speed train with travel times as fast as 1-2 hours. The high-speed train is comfortable, convenient, and a great way to cover long distances quickly.

One of the best things about traveling by train is the stunning views you'll see along the way. From the rolling hills of Tuscany to the dramatic coastline of the Amalfi Coast, you'll be treated to some of the most beautiful scenery in Europe.

Another advantage of traveling by train is that you don't have to worry about traffic or parking, and you can relax and enjoy the journey without the stress of driving.

When planning your train travel, it's a good idea to book your tickets in advance, especially for high-speed trains, as they can sell out quickly. You can book tickets online or at the train station.

High-speed trains tickets: Italo

All the other train tickets TrenItalia: Frecciarossa Frecciaargento locals and intercity

High-speed paths in our journey

Firenze Roma Napoli By Train

High-speed trains are extremely convenient for traveling in Italy, especially on our 10-day journey through the Italian central region. The high-speed trains connect Florence, Rome, and Naples (the largest city near the Amalfi Coast). In fact, it will take just under 1:30 hours to travel from Florence to Rome, a little over 3 hours from Florence to Naples, and one 1 and 20 minutes from Rome to Naples. As a point of reference, Rome and Naples are 470 kilometers apart, which is approximately 292 miles. If we were to drive this distance on the highway, it would take at least five hours.

Tickets can be purchased online or at the station, and the cost varies depending on the type of train and class of service.
When traveling by train in Italy, it's important to remember to validate your ticket before boarding the train using the machines located on the platform. This will avoid any fines or penalties. Also, it's recommended to book your tickets in advance to get the best prices and to secure your seat, especially during peak travel periods.

What are Frecciarossa, Frecciargento, and Italo?

Frecciarossa, Frecciargento, and Italo are **high-speed trains** that operate in Italy. They are some of the fastest and most modern trains in the country and offer a fast and convenient way to travel between major cities.

Here's a brief overview of each of these train services:

Frecciarossa: Frecciarossa is the flagship high-speed train service of Trenitalia, the Italian national railway company. It operates on the Milan-Rome-Naples route and other major cities, including Florence, Bologna, Turin, and Venice. The trains can reach speeds of up to 300 km/h and offer a range of services, including first and second-class seating, Wi-Fi, and a dining car.

Frecciargento: Frecciargento is another high-speed train service operated by Trenitalia, which operates on several routes, including Rome-Venice, Milan-Venice, and Rome-Lecce. It is slightly slower than Frecciarossa but still offers fast travel times and a range of services, including first and second-class seating, Wi-Fi, and a dining car.

Italo: Italo is a private high-speed train operator in Italy, which offers services on the Milan-Naples route and other major cities, including Rome, Florence, and Turin. The trains can reach speeds of up to 300 km/h and offer a range of services, including four different seating classes, Wi-Fi, and a cinema car. Italo is known for its modern and stylish design, as well as its competitive pricing.

All of these high-speed train services offer a fast and convenient way to travel between the biggest cities in Italy, with fast travel times and a range of onboard services. It's important to note that each service has its own ticketing system, and it's recommended to book in advance to secure the best prices and seating options.

What are the differences between high-speed trains vs local regional or intercity?

High-speed trains, such as Frecciarossa, Frecciargento, and Italo in Italy, are designed to provide fast and efficient transportation between major cities. They typically operate on dedicated high-speed rail lines and can reach speeds of up to 300 km/h, allowing passengers to cover long distances quickly.

Local, regional, and intercity trains, on the other hand, typically operate on standard rail lines and make more frequent stops. They are designed to serve local and regional communities and provide transportation between smaller towns and cities. These trains are usually slower than high-speed trains, with maximum speeds of around 160 km/h.

Here are some of the key differences between high-speed trains and local/regional/intercity trains:

1. Speed: High-speed trains are significantly faster than local/regional/intercity trains. They can travel at speeds of up to 300 km/h, while local/regional/intercity trains usually travel at speeds of around 160 km/h or less.
2. Distance: High-speed trains are designed to cover long distances quickly, while local/regional/intercity trains are used for shorter journeys and serve local and regional communities.
3. Frequency: Local/regional/intercity trains usually make more frequent stops than high-speed trains, with some trains making stops at almost every station along the route. High-speed trains typically make fewer stops and are designed for long-distance travel.
4. Comfort: High-speed trains usually offer more comfortable seating and amenities than local/regional/intercity trains. High-speed trains may have more spacious seats, more legroom, Wi-Fi, power outlets, and dining cars.
5. Price: High-speed trains are often more expensive than local/regional/intercity trains, due to their faster travel times and higher level of comfort and amenities. Local/regional/intercity trains are usually more affordable, making them a good option for budget-conscious travelers.

Overall, the choice between high-speed trains and local/regional/intercity trains depends on the traveler's specific needs and budget. High-speed trains are ideal for long-distance travel between major cities, while local/regional/intercity trains are better for shorter journeys and serving local and regional communities.

CAR RENTAL

Before deciding to rent a car, it's important to be aware that Italians have a reputation for aggressive driving!

There are many car rental options available in Italy, but some of the best options include
- **Europcar**: Europcar is a well-known car rental company that operates in Italy and offers a wide range of vehicles to suit different needs and budgets. They have rental locations in major cities and airports across Italy and offer competitive rates and good customer service.
- **Hertz**: Hertz is another popular car rental company in Italy, with locations in major cities and airports throughout the country. They offer a range of vehicles, including luxury cars, and have competitive pricing and good customer service.
- **Avis**: Avis is a well-known car rental company that operates in Italy and offers a range of vehicles, including economy and luxury cars. They have rental locations in major cities and airports across Italy and offer competitive rates and good customer service.
- **Sixt**: Sixt is a German car rental company that has a strong presence in Italy, with rental locations in major cities and airports throughout the country. They offer a

range of vehicles, including luxury cars, and have competitive pricing and good customer service.
- **Budget**: Budget is a global car rental company that operates in Italy and offers a range of vehicles to suit different needs and budgets. They have rental locations in major cities and airports across Italy and offer competitive rates and good customer service.

Car rental companies in Italy are required by law to provide basic insurance coverage with every rental, which typically includes third-party liability insurance and theft protection. However, this basic coverage may not be sufficient for all situations, and additional insurance options are often available.

Before renting a car in Italy, it's essential to review the insurance options available and decide whether additional coverage is needed. Some car rental companies offer additional insurance options, such as collision damage waiver (CDW) and personal accident insurance, which can provide greater protection and peace of mind. However, these additional options may come at an extra cost.

It's also worth noting that credit card companies often provide insurance coverage for rental cars, so it's a good idea to check with your credit card provider to see what coverage is offered and whether it's sufficient for your needs.

In any case, it's important to carefully review the rental agreement and understand the insurance coverage and any associated costs before renting a car in Italy. This can help avoid any surprises or unexpected expenses in the event of an accident or other issues.

Italian highways want to know.

To guarantee smooth travel, navigating Italy's **Autostrade (highways)** demands some expertise, nothing too complicated, but you need to know.

Highway Tolls: In Italy, there are tolls on the roads. **You will be given a ticket** with your entry point indicated on it when you first enter the highway. Upon exiting, you pay the toll according to the total number of kilometers traveled. You can pay with cash, a card, or a **Telepass**. (I kind of Ez-Pass or a Sunpass). You will be charged for the admission point that is farthest from your exit, so it is imperative that you keep your ticket safe.

Speed Limits: In Italy, the posted speed limit on highways **is 130 km/h**, with a reduction to 110 km/h during precipitation. New drivers, or those with less than three years on their license, are not allowed to go faster than 100 km/h. Be advised that **speed** restrictions are strictly **enforced by cameras** and that automatic fines are imposed (and if you're renting a car, sent to car rental companies).

Electric Vehicles: Free green station recharging is available for drivers of electric vehicles on the highways. But at the moment, these stations are only available in specific locations.

Free Wi-Fi Access: Although free Wi-Fi is not available everywhere in Italy, it is available at any **autogrill (service area)** beside the road. To begin browsing, simply establish a connection with the "**Autostrade per l'Italia** Free Wi-Fi" network and adhere to the prompts.

Emergency Services and Rest places: There are rest places spaced out for breaks along the roadway. When there is an emergency, follow the emergency lanes and seek for the S.O.S. columns spaced every two kilometers. With the use of GSM technology, you can contact the Information Radio Center Operator for assistance in case of mechanical or medical emergencies.

Autogrill Stops: Autogrills are more than simply standard rest areas; they also serve **delicious coffee, sandwiches, and trinkets**. They're an excellent location for a quick bite to eat and refuel your vehicle. I still remember my favorite Panino of the Autogrill. You should try it: the Camogli!

Refueling Advice: The autostrada's filling facilities are self-serve and simple to operate. Make sure your credit card has a PIN or have a backup debit card ready because Italy employs a PIN-based credit card system for payments.

Recognizing Road Signs: Get acquainted with Italian road signs, as they may not resemble your own. Road signs employ symbols and are written in Italian. For instance, a sign stating that in foggy conditions, the speed limit is 40 km/h. Keep in mind that traffic signs won't be in English, so familiarizing yourself with these symbols before you go is essential.

Lane discipline: Stay in the right lane if you're moving more slowly or aren't actively passing. Left lanes are for vehicles that are going quicker or passing. Unfortunately, not so many Italians remember this rule, but it's a good thing to know it!

Following these recommendations will make driving on Italy's autostrade safer and more pleasurable. Recall that preparation and knowledge of local driving customs are essential for a stress-free trip.

BY PLANE

Low-Cost Airlines

If you're looking to travel on a budget in Italy, there are several low-cost airline options available. Here are a few things to know about these airlines:

- **Ryanair**: Ryanair is an Irish low-cost airline that operates flights throughout Europe, including many destinations in Italy. Ryanair is known for its low fares and no-frills service, with extra fees for things like checked luggage and seat selection. It's important to carefully read the terms and conditions and understand any fees before booking a flight with Ryanair.
- **easyJet**: easyJet is a British low-cost airline that operates flights to many destinations in Italy, including Rome, Milan, Naples, and Venice. Like Ryanair, easyJet is known for its low fares and no-frills service, with extra fees for things like checked luggage and seat selection.
- **Wizz Air**: Wizz Air is a Hungarian low-cost airline that operates flights to several destinations in Italy, including Rome, Naples, and Bari. Wizz Air is known for its low fares and focus on Eastern European destinations, with Additional charges that may apply for services such as checked baggage and preferred seating.
- **Volotea**: Volotea is a Spanish low-cost airline that operates flights to several destinations in Italy, including Venice, Naples, and Palermo. Volotea is known for its low fares and focuses on smaller, regional destinations, with extra fees for things like checked luggage and seat selection.

It's important to note **that low-cost airlines** often have **stricter baggage allowances**, so it's essential to check the airline's website and understand their baggage policy before booking a flight. Additionally, low-cost airlines often have additional fees for things like checked luggage, seat selection, and onboard meals, so it's important to read the terms and conditions and understand any fees before booking a flight.

Airports

Italy has several major airports that serve both domestic and international destinations. Here are some of the busiest and most important airports in Italy:

- Leonardo da Vinci Fiumicino Airport (FCO): Located near Rome, Fiumicino Airport is the busiest airport in Italy, handling over 40 million passengers per year. It is a hub for Alitalia, Italy's national airline, as well as several other airlines, and offers non-stop flights to destinations around the world.
- Malpensa Airport (MXP): Located near Milan, Malpensa Airport is Italy's second-busiest airport, handling over 20 million passengers per year. It is a hub for several airlines, including Alitalia, and offers non-stop flights to destinations around the world.
- Marco Polo Airport (VCE): Located near Venice, Marco Polo Airport is one of Italy's busiest airports, handling over 11 million passengers per year. It is a hub for several airlines, including Volotea and easyJet, and offers non-stop flights to destinations around Europe and beyond.
- Naples International Airport (NAP): Located in southern Italy, Naples International Airport is a major hub for southern Italy and the island of Sicily. It offers non-stop flights to destinations throughout Italy, as well as several international destinations.
- Bologna Guglielmo Marconi Airport (BLQ): Located in northern Italy, Bologna Airport is a major hub for the Emilia-Romagna region. It offers non-stop flights to destinations throughout Italy and Europe, as well as several long-haul destinations.

These are just a few of the major airports in Italy, and there are many others, including airports in Florence, Turin, Palermo, and more.

DAY 1 AND 2 AND 3
ROMA

TRANSPORTATION

Navigating through Rome can be a real challenge. The city's sprawling landscape, congested traffic, and, not to forget, the condition of the roads all contribute to a less-than-ideal transportation experience. **And for the love of espresso, please reconsider if you're considering renting a car**—please don't do it!

So, how should you navigate this ancient metropolis? Fear not, because we've got you covered with top-notch advice on the best ways to get around Rome.

FROM AND TO THE FIUMICINO INTERNATIONAL AIRPORT

The Rome Fiumicino Airport is located just 32 km from the capital and has good connections to Rome's city center via buses and trains.
The best option is by express train:

The non-stop Leonardo Express train to Rome Termini Station travels from Leonardo da Vinci Airport to Rome Termini in 32 minutes without intermediate stops.
It departs every 15 minutes during the pick hours; otherwise, it leaves every 30 minutes.
The first train from Rome Termini departs at 5:50 AM and the last at 10:50 PM from platforms 23 and 24.

From Fiumicino Airport, the first train leaves at 6:38 AM and the last at 11:38 PM.
On the Trenitalia website, a ticket for the Leonardo Express costs 14 euros each way and is guaranteed even in the event of a strike.

HANDY TIPS & SUGGESTIONS

First, Rome's iconic landmarks are spread across a large area, but the good news is that most **are accessible by foot.** If you're new to the city, we highly recommend starting off with a walking tour; alternatively, you can hop on a tourist bus for a panoramic overview of the capital—ideal for those 'wow' Instagram moments and familiarize yourself with the layout of the city.

But the best way is definitely using the subway. It's cheap and when is open (sometimes you will find that they have tricky schedules, especially during the central two weeks of August)
There are several ticket options. I suggest the daily pass: 24h €7.00, but there are also 48-hour and 72-hour options.

ELECTRIC SCOOTERS THE FUTURE IS HERE!

Are you Feeling tired or in a spot far from train stations? Don't fret; you've got a fabulous option—rent an electric scooter! These handy little machines are scattered throughout the city and cost a mere €0.15 per minute. Payment is a cinch, too, thanks to options like Apple Pay and PayPal. All you need to do is scan the scooter's QR code to start your ride. Just a heads-up: don't forget to disconnect the scooter when you're done.

ROMA BIKE SHARING

If cycling's more your speed, check out Rome's city-run bike-sharing program. Use their handy app to find one of the 78 stations across the city. The app lets you register, unlock bikes, and buy a €10 payment card, which you can top up directly in the app. Ride costs? Just €0.50 per half-hour.

Taxis are an alternative, but beware: they're pretty **pricey**, and, yes, they also get caught in that infamous Roman traffic.

But if, for any reason, you're determined to drive and run the car, be really careful with the Limit Traffic Zone (ZTL) and parking tickets!

UNDERSTANDING THE FOUNDATION OF ROME

THE SEVEN HILLS

To begin our journey through Rome, we must start with a foundational understanding. Over our immersive three-day adventure, I often reference a set of **7 hills**. These aren't just any hills; they are the bedrock upon which the ancient city of Rome was meticulously constructed. Grasping the layout of Rome and maneuvering through its intricate pathways requires a fundamental acquaintance with these hills. For clarity and a touch of authenticity, I'll be referring to them by their Italian names.

The esteemed seven hills of Rome are:

- Palatino (Palatine) • Aventino (Aventine) • Campidoglio (Capitoline) • Quirinale (Quirinal) • Viminale (Viminal) • Esquilino (Esquiline) • Celio (Caelian)

Armed with this knowledge, you'll find yourself well-prepared to embark on a journey that showcases Rome's beauty and provides a deeper appreciation for its storied past and breathtaking landscapes.

In this guide, you'll find several QR codes **to enhance your exploration**.

While wandering through **Rome, you'll find 2 QR codes**: one focuses on the city's **illustrious landmarks**, while the other whisks you away to culinary delights, introducing you to **the best of Roman food and eateries**.

I strongly advise you to become well-acquainted with Rome's map. Familiarity with the locations and orientation of the seven hills is instrumental for flawless navigation and a truly immersive experience within the city.

ANCIENT ROME'S MYTHOLOGY

In the earliest tales of Rome, twin brothers named Romulus and Remus played a big part. According to legend, after their royal parents were overthrown, the twins were thrown into the River Tiber but were saved by a she-wolf who cared for them. As they grew older and learned of their royal roots, they wanted to establish a city. However, they disagreed on its location. In the end, Romulus founded the city and named it Rome after himself. That's how the story says Rome began!

When discussing Rome, I've noticed that many, including myself, often get mixed up about the various eras of the Roman Empire. To provide clarity, I'd like to briefly touch upon the mythology that birthed the Roman Empire, as well as its three pivotal periods: the Monarchy, the Republic, and the Empire. Understanding these aspects will greatly enhance your visit to Rome, helping you discern the significance of each monument, its historical context, and the story behind it.

HISTORY OF THE ROMAN EMPIRE

The vast history of the Roman Empire can be segmented into distinct periods, each with its unique developments and characteristics. Let's delve into this chronology to gain a clearer understanding:

1. The Monarchy (circa 753-509 BC): This era commenced with the legendary founding of Rome by Romulus in 753 BC. During this time, Rome was ruled by a succession of seven kings. This period saw the establishment of foundational institutions and the city's initial expansion.

2. The Republic (509-31 BC or 509-27 BC): The Republican era began in 509 BC when the last Roman king was overthrown, leading to the establishment of the Roman Republic. This period lasted until the Battle of Actium in 31 BC, or alternatively, until 27 BC when the Roman Senate bestowed full powers and the title of 'Augustus' upon Octavian. This era witnessed Rome's growth into a dominant Mediterranean power, driven by military conquests, infrastructure development, and sociopolitical reforms.

3. The Empire (31 or 27 BC - 476 AD): Starting either from the Battle of Actium in 31 BC or from 27 BC when Octavian became Augustus, the Imperial age spanned until 476 AD. This marked the year when Romulus Augustulus, the last Roman emperor of the West, was deposed. Throughout this period, the empire expanded its territories exponentially, reaching its zenith in terms of territorial expanse, culture, and architectural feats.

By understanding these periods and their corresponding dates, you'll be better equipped to grasp the rich tapestry of Rome's history, enabling a deeper appreciation of its legacy and the remnants that still stand today.

DAY 1
ANCIENT ROME

ROMA

There's no doubt that a lifetime wouldn't be enough to uncover all the marvels Rome has to offer. However, if you're planning a quick three-day whirlwind tour of this magnificent city, having a well-thought-out itinerary can be a game-changer. Trust us, we've got a fantastic one lined up for you! With our plan, you won't miss out on any of the city's must-see attractions, museums, or iconic landmarks. Brace yourselves for an unforgettable Roman adventure!

Before we dive into your Roman escapade, here's a golden tip to save you valuable time—always buy your tickets online before you arrive. Trust me, it's worth it, and you'll thank yourself for avoiding the often frustrating long lines.

Let's kick off our journey with none other than the world-renowned Colosseum, one of Rome's defining symbols.

We recommend starting your day bright and early to dodge the crowds. **Don't forget to pack a water bottle, and don't buy them in front of the sites** often; the "sellers" are not authorized. Keep your bottle. There are several water-free fountains all over the city where you can refill your bottle.

COLOSSEUM

As you emerge from the Colosseum subway station, the colossal amphitheater appears right in front of you, and the first word that will likely come to mind is 'breathtaking.' It's not just an iconic symbol of Rome, but it's also a window into ancient history and Roman engineering marvels. If you're going to Rome, this is an absolute must-visit; there's no two ways about it.

Colosseo

THE HISTORY

Constructed under the Flavian dynasty (also known as the Flavian Amphitheatre), initiated by Emperor Vespasian in 72 AD and later completed by his son Titus in 80 AD, the Colosseum is steeped in history. The 100-day-long inaugural ceremony, during which 5,000 animals were sacrificed, marked its completion. This grand amphitheater could accommodate more than 50,000 spectators, who gathered to watch gladiator fights, mock naval battles, and other public spectacles.

This iconic structure, part of the UNESCO World Heritage site since 1980 and named one of the New Seven Wonders of the World in 2007

Interesting fact: did you know that the Colosseum, even in its ancient times, had the capability to be covered, much like modern stadiums today? Picture this: there were hundreds of tents that could cover the entire central arena.

Colosseo

TIPS FOR YOUR VISIT

Lines to get into this historical marvel can stretch for what seems like miles. So here's a pro tip: buy your tickets online in advance; this will save you hours, I promise!
On my website, you can find regular tickets or guided tours.
www.italyunveiled.com

WHAT'S INSIDE?

Once you're in, prepare to be transported back in time. The architecture and engineering are jaw-dropping, to say the least. The Colosseum was ingeniously designed with a complex system of tunnels, trap doors, and elevators used for animals and gladiators into the arena. Although much of the original structure has suffered from the ravages of time and human activity, what remains is enough to paint a vivid picture of its grandeur.

IL PALATINO - PALATINE HILL

Don't just stop at the Colosseum; the surrounding area is replete with sites that add context and depth to your visit. Right next to it is the Arco di Costantino, or **Arch of Constantine**, built to commemorate Emperor Constantine's victory over Maxentius. A little further is **Palatine Hill,** one of Rome's 7 hills, filled with the ruins of ancient palaces.

Ascend the historic **Palatine Hill** and you step onto the ground where Rome's story is believed to have begun. It's here, enveloped in **layers of legend and archaeological treasures**, that the city's foundation myths come to life. Tradition holds that the Palatine is where **Romulus and Remus, the twin founders of Rome**, were nurtured by the she-wolf in the shelter of a cave, a tale as enduring as the city itself.

Archaeological finds support the narrative of the **Palatine as the birthplace of Rome**, revealing that the earliest Roman community settled upon its slopes. As you explore, imagine the Palatine in its imperial heyday—a neighborhood of emperors, a place where power and luxury converged.

The House of Livia, (casa di Livia) named for the wife of Emperor Augustus, offers a glimpse into the imperial life with its remarkably preserved frescoes and **mosaics**. Although the most brilliant mosaics have been removed, they continue to tell the story of the grandeur that once adorned these walls from their new home in the National Roman Museum. This museum, conveniently located near the bustling Termini Station, safeguards these treasures, allowing a broader audience to appreciate the intricate artistry of ancient Rome.

ROMAN FORUM

Via dei Fori Imperiali to the Foro Romano (Roman Forum), once the bustling heart of ancient Rome.

Foro Romano

In ancient Rome, the **Foro Romano** was the city's vibrant hub, filled with shops, courts, and temples. The Forum's significance faded over time, but archaeological digs in the 19th and 20th centuries unveiled its wonders.

Across the street lies the archaeological complex of the **Via dei Fori Imperiali** (Imperial Fora), built by various emperors between 42 and 112 BC, such As Giulio Cesare, Augusto, Vespasiano, etc.

Visiting the Foro Romano and Fori Imperiali is important for understanding Rome's ancient heritage. The Roman Forum, nestled between Rome's iconic Campidoglio and Palatino hills, was once a center for trade, politics, and religious events, resonating with the rich tapestry of Roman life.

RIONE MONTI

As you journey down Via dei Fori Imperiali and turn onto Via Cavour, you'll find yourself stepping into the very heart of Rome's oldest district, Rione Monti.

This enchanting neighborhood, historically working-class, remains one of the city's most authentic and charismatic areas. Indeed, Monti retains a touch of its original inhabitants—the Monticiani, true-blooded Romans who are proud of their roots (I can attest to this since my father was born and raised right here!).

Draped behind the iconic Colosseum, Monti's charming maze of winding streets and alleys has, remarkably, escaped the typical tourist traps. Instead, it's flourished, cultivating an independent spirit that makes it one of the liveliest and most invigorating districts in the capital. It has metamorphosed into **Rome's bohemian and hipster hub**, brimming with artists, artisans, intellectuals, affluent students, and night owls who appreciate a good evening out.

Now, when in Monti, experiencing the evening ritual of an **aperitivo in Piazza Madonna dei Monti** is essential.

Especially during the summertime, the square pulsates with so much life that you might find it challenging to navigate through the bustling crowd. Don't miss the chance to **visit the Basilica di San Pietro in Vincoli** either. It's not only home to the tomb of Julius II, boasting **Michelangelo's renowned Moses**, but it also shelters the chains believed to have bound Saint Peter in the Mamertine Prison.

And for those always on the hunt for gastronomic delights, here's a fun tidbit: **Via del Boschetto** holds the title for the street with the **highest density of restaurants per square meter in Rome**! Quite the feat for a city bursting with culinary treasures.

PIAZZA VENEZIA E CAMPIDOGLIO

Making your way back to Via dei Fori Imperiali, take a left turn onto Via di S. Pietro in Carcere. As you journey along, you'll pass under the renowned **sculpture of the she-wolf nursing Romulus and Remus**, an emblematic symbol of the city.

Following this path will lead you straight to the stunning **Piazza del Campidoglio.** This square, beautifully adorned with buildings designed by the genius Michelangelo, is home to Rome's City Hall and the famed **Capitoline Museums**. Given its artistic and historical importance, it's no wonder it's considered one of Rome's most exquisite squares. Take a moment to admire the intricately designed floor pattern—it's truly a masterpiece.

Altare della patria - Vittoriano

Venturing down its grand staircase, you'll spot another set of stairs, slightly steeper, leading to the **Basilica of Santa Maria in Ara Coeli.** At the base of both stairways, you'll find yourself in the iconic **Piazza Venezia. Here, the imposing monument of Vittoriano** stands majestically, capturing every visitor's gaze. Conceived in 1885 to celebrate the Unification of Italy, the monument is now a tribute to the Unknown Soldier.

And for a breathtaking panoramic view of Rome, **I highly recommend making the ascent to the top terrace**. From there, you'll be treated to an almost 360-degree visual feast of the Eternal City. It's a perspective of Rome that is both awe-inspiring and memorable!

TREVI FOUNTAIN

Leave Piazza Venezia behind you, stroll down the bustling **Via del Corso** and you'll find your way to the iconic **Fontana di Trevi.** Immortalized by Fellini's masterpiece, "La Dolce Vita", this magnificent fountain stands as Rome's most lavish and extensive water feature.

Fontana di Trevi

Nestled against the backdrop of an architectural wonder, a time-honored tradition beckons visitors. Turning your back to the fountain and casting a coin over your shoulder is believed to ensure a return trip to the Eternal City.

Although the square accommodating this grand structure is surprisingly compact and often swarmed with tourists, participating in this ritual is a quintessential Roman experience. For those seeking a serene moment, consider visiting early morning, during the late evening, or at night. Under the glow of lights, the newly restored shimmering white marble glistens, and the square often finds its peace.

A stone's throw away, opposite Via del Corso, you'll discover **Piazza Colonna**. Here, you can admire the striking **Column of Marcus Aurelius** and the prestigious **Palazzo Chigi**, home to Italy's Prime Minister.

PIAZZA DI SPAGNA – SPANISH STEPS

Strolling away from Fontana di Trevi, your next stop should undoubtedly be **Piazza di Spagna**. Venturing north via Via della Stamperia, the **Spanish Steps**, or as the locals call them, **"Scalinata di Trinità dei Monti",** soon appear in all their grandeur.

Built in the first half of the 18th century, these steps owe their name to the Spanish Embassy, which once obviously resided near here. Today, Piazza di Spagna, along with its surrounding streets, buzzes not just with tourists, but also with the lively energy of local teenagers. They often gather here, especially on Saturday afternoons.
As the golden hues of sunset drape the city, ascend the steps to the left. From there, treat yourself to a panoramic view while enjoying an aperitivo, letting Rome's timeless charm wash over you.

DINNER OPTIONS

FOOD IN ROME

After a wonderfully exhaustive day where we have seen and experienced so much, it's time to think about dinner.

After your delightful aperitivo near Piazza di Spagna, and for an authentic Roman experience, I'd recommend hopping in a taxi and heading over to the lively **Trastevere** area.

Alternatively, you might consider embarking on a scenic **cruise along the Tiber River**, offering dinner or perhaps just an aperitivo if you prefer that over the one at Piazza di Spagna. Another delightful option is to revisit the Rione Monti district full of amazing restaurants.

For all meal references, simply scan the QR code included in this guide. It will lead you to a customized Google map I've personally created just for you, pinpointing the best eateries.

I wish you "Buon appetito" and a "Buona notte".
Let's meet again tomorrow for yet another fabulous day in Rome!

DAY 2
Vatican City

Let's kickstart our second day in true Italian style with a delightful breakfast - a rich cappuccino, a flaky brioche, or perhaps a delectable **maritozzo**.
When in Rome, it's almost a ritual to indulge in maritozzi!

Our first destination might seem like we're leaving the city, but it's just a playful jest.
In reality, we're venturing into **the world's smallest state nestled right within Rome: the Vatican City!**
If you've browsed any of my other guides, you'll know that I always advocate for visiting significant churches in Italy, regardless of one's religious beliefs.
These churches are treasure troves of unparalleled art, with world-renowned artists contributing to their construction and intricate designs. And, of course, St. Peter's Basilica, the epitome of Christendom, is no exception to this rule.

Now, let me give you a heads-up.
Whether it's the Basilica, the museums, or the Sistine Chapel, brace yourself for quite the queue, so get your tickets in advance. This way, you effortlessly bypass those winding lines.

BASILICA DI SAN PIETRO

The Basilica is an architectural wonder, standing as the largest church in the world (some people would argue that is the second biggest because they consider the volume and not the surface). Regardless of one's religious beliefs, the monument's magnificence is breathtaking.

Bramante, Raphael, Michelangelo... oh, the legendary names that contributed to this marvel!

While Bramante and Raphael had their touches, it's Michelangelo's brilliance that often steals the show.

Just think of that iconic dome or the touching **"Pietà"** greeting you as you step into the right nave. It's art in its purest form. But, of course, the wonders don't end inside.

Step out to **the Piazza San Pietro and let Bernini's iconic colonnade** envelope you with its grandeur.

View of Vatican City from the top of Saint Peter Basilica

Want a bird's eye view? Head up to the dome. While an elevator gets you partway, the rest is a bit of an adventure on foot. But trust me, the sights from up there—overlooking the square and the Vatican gardens—are nothing short of breathtaking.

There's a separate ticket for this view. And if you're here on a Wednesday and hold faith close to your heart, there's a chance to attend the Pope's audience. Just remember to book in advance.

MUSEI VATICANI E CAPPELLA SISTINA

As you step into the Vatican Museums, you'll find yourself surrounded by a breathtaking collection of artistic treasures. The vastness of the space is truly awe-inspiring, and to fully appreciate every artifact and masterpiece, you would need more than just a couple of days.

But there are numerous rooms and paintings that are simply outstanding and shouldn't be missed.
One such highlight is **the Raphael's Rooms** – commonly called "Le Stanze" which showcases grand frescoes by Raphael. Initially, apartments for Pope Julius II were crafted to eclipse his predecessor's quarters. Spanning four rooms, including the famous **Sala di Costantino**, their completion extended beyond Raphael's passing in 1520.
As you explore the rooms, you'll be mesmerized by the intricate artwork of the great **Raffaello Sanzio**. Every brushstroke tells a story of a bygone era, transporting you to a different time and place.

Vatican museum

Not too far away lies one of the world's marvels, which, in my opinion, boasts the most beautiful painting ever made - **the Sistine Chapel (Cappella Sistina in Italian)**.
The canvas painted by the legendary **Michelangelo** on its ceiling offers a celestial spectacle, with sheer brilliance and attention to detail that makes it seem as though you're standing beneath a heavenly sky.
Originally named "the Cappella Magna," it was built between 1473 and 1481 under Pope Sixtus IV. Michelangelo painted the ceiling from 1508 to 1512. Today, it remains one of the most important tourist attractions and a central religious site, as well as the location for the papal conclave.

To maximize your experience and dive deeper into the treasures, **I'd recommend opting for a 3-hour guided tour** that covers the Vatican Museums, Sistine Chapel, and St. Peter's Basilica. Trust me, those three hours, rich in art and history, guided by an expert, elevate the experience to a whole new level.

CASTEL SANT'ANGELO

As you meander along the Tiber River bank, one landmark that will undoubtedly catch your eye is **Castel Sant'Angelo**.
Indeed, no trip to Rome would be complete without a visit!
Originally constructed as Emperor Adriano's mausoleum, by the 6th century, this iconic structure was repurposed into a papal fortress.

Castel Sant'Angelo

To this day, it houses the famed **"passetto"** – a secretive passageway that connects the castle to St. Peter's Basilica, serving as a refuge for popes in times of peril.

If your schedule permits, I highly recommend exploring the museum nestled within its walls. And, do yourself a favor: ascend to its terraces for a breathtaking panoramic view over Rome's rooftops.
As you depart Castel Sant'Angelo, take a leisurely walk across **Ponte degli Angeli (**the Bridge of Angels). The bridge gets its

name from the exquisite angel sculptures adorning it, masterfully crafted by students of the renowned artist, **Bernini.**

PIAZZA NAVONA

Once you've crossed the bridge, follow Via dei Coronari, and it'll lead you straight to the historical Piazza Navona.

With its Roman roots, the square's intriguing name hints at its past when it was occasionally flooded to host mock naval battles.

For over three centuries, this bustling square was the heartbeat of the city, home to its main market.
Today, it's a vibrant tapestry of street performers, artists, fortune tellers, and characters, all eager to engage with curious travelers.

Piazza Navona

Don't miss **Bernini's majestic Fountain of the Four Rivers (dei quattro fiumi)**, with the equally impressive **Church of Sant'Agnese** in Agone designed by Borromini standing right across.

Piazza Navona also hosts Rome's most beloved **Christmas market,** and it's a local tradition for Romans to flock here on the Epiphany, January 6th.

Just a stone's throw away, you'll find **the Bramante Cloister**, currently used as an exhibition space – and let me tell you, they often curate some truly captivating exhibits there!

THE PANTHEON

It's merely a short walk before you're greeted by the breathtaking **Piazza della Rotonda**, housing the **Pantheon**.

This historical marvel, arguably one of the most gorgeous spots in Rome, boasts unparalleled beauty, both inside and out.

Its awe-inspiring dome, a testament to ancient Roman architectural prowess, served as an inspiration for Michelangelo when designing the dome of St. Peter's Basilica.

The oculus is a grand circular opening at the very center of its iconic dome, measuring 8.9 meters (more than 29 feet) in diameter. This architectural marvel not only serves as the primary source of natural light for the interior but also symbolizes the connection between the temple and the heavens above.

Initially a Roman temple, the Pantheon was consecrated as a church in 609 AD. Venture inside to witness the grand tombs of Vittorio Emanuele II, Umberto I, and the renowned artist Raffaello.

Pantheon

Just behind the Pantheon's square, take a moment to glimpse at **Piazza della Minerva**. Dominating the scene is an intriguing statue: an original Egyptian obelisk gracefully carried on the back of a white marble elephant. Additionally, the Church of St. Maria Sopra Minerva here houses exquisite frescoes by Filippino Lippi and a remarkable sculpture by Michelangelo.

For caffeine enthusiasts like me, this district is home to Rome's most celebrated coffee roaster and bar: **Casa del Caffè Tazza d'Oro**.
And if you're wandering these streets during summer, ditch the classic espresso for a refreshing coffee granita topped with cream. It's simply divine!

CAMPO DÈ FIORI and GHETTO

Just a short walk across Corso Vittorio Emanuele will lead you to Campo dei Fiori, a beloved square by the locals. By day, it hosts a lively fruit and vegetable market, while evenings see it filled with the youth at the many outdoor bars. Dominating the square's center is the statue of Giordano Bruno, martyred here for heresy in 1600.

Continue straight on Via dei Giubbonari to reach Rome's ancient **Jewish Ghetto.**

This distinctive part of central Rome blends remnants of Roman and medieval homes, offering plenty of trattorias serving authentic Roman dishes, such as the famous **"carciofi alla giudia"** (so delicious)
The heart of the Ghetto is the **Portico d'Ottavia**, built by Augustus, which, from the Middle Ages until the late 19th century, was Rome's fish market.

Nearby stands the **Tempio Maggiore**, Rome's first monumental synagogue, built in 1904, housing the **Museum of Jewish Art**. If you're intrigued by the history of this neighborhood, consider joining a tour that explores both the Jewish Ghetto and Trastevere, lasting 3 hours and offering an insightful experience

L'ISOLA TIBERINA

Tiber Island, hidden in the heart of the Tiber River, is an enchanting place brimming with history and charm.

Directly opposite the Synagogue, you can access the island via the **Ponte Fabricio, the oldest Roman bridge still in use today**.

The island, the only urban one on the Tiber, is home to the Fatebenefratelli Hospital, a healing place that has served the Roman community since the 1500s. You'll also find the Israelite Hospital and a few picturesque homes.

One of the highlights of the island is the historic **Trattoria Sora Lella**. Sora Lella, (sora means sister in Roman dialect), whose real name was Elena Fabrizi, was an iconic figure in the Roman culinary scene and also a well-known character in the Italian entertainment industry. She was famous not only for her restaurant but also for her memorable roles in various Italian films and TV programs during the 1980s.

Her trattoria, which opened in 1940, quickly became a Roman institution, famed for serving traditional Roman dishes. **My suggestion is definitely to have dinner here.**

Spaghetti carbonara

Strolling southward, the remains of the first stone bridge of ancient Rome, known as **Ponte Rotto**, will offer you a captivating glimpse into Roman history. If you wish to explore further, the Ponte Cestio will lead you directly to the vibrant neighborhood of **Trastevere**, located on the other side of the Tiber.

Beyond its rich history, Tiber Island is also a gathering spot during the summer. Locals and tourists alike enjoy outdoor events, like film screenings and market stalls, which transform the island into a hub of cultural activity. The mix of history, culture, and ambiance makes Tiber Island a must-visit for anyone traveling to Rome.

AN EVENING IN TRASTEVERE

As the sun casts its golden hues over Rome and the day begins to mellow, consider saving the best of your energies for an immersive evening in the timeless Trastevere. This is when the day's itinerary becomes less about checking off sites and more about feeling the city's heartbeat.

Trastevere

Start by meandering up the slopes of the **Gianicolo hill**. A gentle climb, but well worth the effort, this hill is a local favorite for its breathtaking panoramas of the Eternal City.

As the terracotta rooftops stretch beneath, the iconic structures of Rome— the Colosseum, St. Peter's Basilica, and the Roman Forum— stand proudly in the distance, silhouetted against the twilight sky.

Here, atop the Gianicolo, stands an age-old cannon, a remnant of times gone by. Every day since 1904, this cannon has offered a unique midday spectacle, firing a blank shot at precisely noon. This tradition continues as a link between Rome's present and its storied past.

Trastevere

After the captivating vistas from Gianicolo, descend into the maze-like lanes of Trastevere.

Cobbled streets, lined with ancient buildings bathed in the warm glow of street lamps, guide your way. Once considered the heart of working-class Rome, **Trastevere** wears its history on its sleeve. **The district's name itself, translating to "across the Tiber,"** speaks of its location and the distinct cultural flavor it cultivated, being set apart from the main hustle and bustle of central Rome.

Trastevere

While today's Trastevere might be a blend of old and new, with a mix of lifelong residents and international newcomers, it hasn't lost its authentic charm. The echoes of laughter, the clinking of glasses, and the aroma of hearty Roman dishes fill the air as trattorias and wine bars come alive. Whether you're seeking a plate of classic "cacio e pepe" or a contemporary twist on Roman delicacies, Trastevere has a seat at the table for you.

Strolling through Trastevere in the evening and witnessing the rest of Rome lit up in all its splendor is an experience not to be missed. So, if you've dined at Sora Lella, come here for a delightful walk afterward. Otherwise, as mentioned earlier, you'll find dozens of other spots for a fabulous dinner.

DAY 3
TESTACCIO, VILLA BORGHESE, CIRCO MASSIMO

We've reached our last day in Rome. I know I've had you run far and wide, so today we'll use the metro a bit to see places that are a little farther apart. I would start with a neighborhood that's unusual for tourists, but if you want the best maritozzo in the city, you must go to Testaccio.

Il Maritozzaro on Via Ettore Rolli 50 is a place you absolutely must visit! In case you don't feel like walking that far, **Pasticceria Linari** in Via Zabagia 9 might be another amazing option. If you opt for this location, make a stop at that Food Market as well.it is a Glass-roofed market on a Roman archeological site with 100+ gourmet & fresh food stalls & more.

Testaccio is definitely more of an everyday life neighborhood with less history compared to the areas we've previously explored. It started as a working-class district but now hosts numerous restaurants, venues, and street art.

The nearest subway stop is **Piramide**.

Once you exit the station, you'll immediately understand the reason for its name. Yes, right in front of you will be a beautiful pyramid. So, after finishing our cappuccino and maritozzo, we're ready for a quick tour to see the Pyramid Cestia, an

Egyptian-style pyramid built in Rome between 18 and 12 B.C. as a tomb for Gaio Cestio Epulone.
Right behind, hidden by walls, there's also the **cimitero acattolico**, considered a sort of secret garden adorned with spectacular tomb sculptures.

Let's hop back on the subway and head to **Villa Borghese**. Take Line B from the Piramide station, transfer at the Termini station, and then switch to Line A. Get off at the Flaminio station.

VILLA BORGHESE

Villa Borghese This is the most famous park in the capital and one of the largest in Europe, Villa Borghese.
Here, Romans come to stroll, play sports, play, or visit one of the various attractions and exhibitions found inside or just outside.
These include the **most famous Galleria Borghese, the Modern and Contemporary Art Gallery, the Cinema Museum, and Villa Giulia's Etruscan Museum.**
Head towards the **Giardino del Lago**, a garden within the garden, with a romantic pond in the center where you can rent a small boat and enjoy a peaceful morning.
From here, go see **the ancient water clock** before arriving at the Terrazza del Pincio.

Villa Borghese

PINCIO AND PIAZZA DEL POPOLO

This terrace owes its name to the Pincio family, who once owned this garden adjacent to Villa Borghese in the 4th century.

The grand terrace is truly magnificent, offering views of Piazza del Popolo, St. Peter's, and half of the city, with the sunset from here being exceptional.
To the left of the terrace is Villa Poniatowski, commonly known by the Romans as Casina Valadier because he designed it in the 1700s for the nephew of the King of Poland.

Descending from the Pincio, you'll find yourself in **Piazza del Popolo,** surrounded by three churches and three fountains by Valadier. At the center of this vast elliptical plaza is the **Flaminio Obelisk, one of Rome's 13 ancient obelisks**.

GALLERIA BORGHESE

If you don't like to spend all this time outdoors, or the weather doesn't allow it, consider dedicating a couple of hours to visiting the **Borghese Gallery**, founded due to Cardinal Scipione Borghese's love for art.
The gallery houses works by **Bernini, Canova, Caravaggio, Raphael, Perugino, and many others**.
The exhibits in the rooms of this neoclassical 19th-century residence are simply astonishing! Here, you can admire Bernini's renowned sculptures of The Rape of Proserpina, Apollo and Daphne, David, and Aeneas and Anchises, as well as Pauline Borghese sculpted by Canova and Boy with a Basket of Fruit by Caravaggio.

*To access the gallery, **you must book and buy tickets in advance** through the official website. Entries are limited, and you'll have 2 hours to explore the entire gallery (which should be sufficient).*

At this point, you might consider taking the metro to reach the Circus Maximus. However, a charming alternative would be to reach this area by navigating the Tiber on a tourist boat.

AVENTINE AND CIRCUS MAXIMUS

Upon exiting the metro, you'll immediately see the remains of the largest entertainment structure ever built by humans.
The Circus Maximus was traditionally dedicated to horse racing and measures a whopping 620 meters in length and 140 meters in width!
Today, it's often used for major events and concerts.

Circus Maximus

Walk along its left side, heading towards the Tiber, and delve into the **Aventine Hill**, one of Rome's most beautiful and sought-after residential areas.

Highlights here include the **Basilica of Santa Sabina** and the **Orange Garden**.
On the same street, in Piazza dei Cavalieri di Malta 3, the famous **"keyhole" offers a stunning view** of St. Peter's dome framed by garden hedges. You'll recognize it immediately by the queue of people waiting.

As dinner time approaches, unfortunately, it's our last in Rome. From here, you're close to everything. Taking the metro, you can reach the Monti district, return to Trastevere, or head back to Testaccio.
By now, you're familiar with the city; after all, you've become a bit Roman too. Tomorrow morning, get ready, as we head to Florence!

DAY 4 AND 5
FIRENZE

FIRENZE

It's time to head to Florence! Italy boasts a truly well-structured **train system**, making the connection between Rome and Florence straightforward. In a little bit more than an hour, and with less than €20 per person, you will be in Florence.

From **Roma Termini**, you'll hop on either the **Frecciarossa** or **Italo** train heading to Firenze Santa Maria Novella.

(To learn more about Italian railroads, check out the end of this guide, where I explain the differences between fast trains and local trains, as well as other modes of transportation).

The journey unfolds amidst the picturesque Italian countryside, where rolling hills and quaint villages provide a serene backdrop to the anticipation bubbling within. As the train glides smoothly along the tracks, the excitement of exploring Florence's historic streets grows with every passing kilometer.

Arriving at Firenze Santa Maria Novella, the city's main train station, you're instantly greeted by a blend of historical charm and modern hustle. This bustling transportation hub, a gateway to the Renaissance, is where your Florentine adventure truly begins.

A BIT OF INTRODUCTION

Florence is a city where the past and the present dance together in a timeless harmony. Even today, as you stroll along its cobblestone streets, you can feel the breath of the Renaissance at every corner. But there's also a modern and dynamic Florence awaiting you, a city that has managed to evolve without losing its historical soul.

The first encounter with the city takes you back in time, with monuments like the **Duomo** and the **Uffizi Gallery** narrating stories of artistic genius and humanism. But beyond these historical icons, there's a vibrant and contemporary Florence inviting you to explore.
Modern art galleries, design shops, trendy cafes, and innovative restaurants blend with traditional artisan shops and classic wine bars, offering a rich and varied cultural and gastronomic panorama.

The culinary scene in Florence is a journey of discovery. On one hand, there's the Tuscan tradition with its authentic and robust flavors, and on the other, innovative chefs reinterpret local cuisine in a modern key, creating unique culinary experiences.

Green parks and open spaces like the **Boboli Gardens** offer a relaxing break from artistic discovery, while local markets like **Sant'Ambrogio Market** allow you to immerse yourself in the daily life of Florence.

And then there's the people. The inhabitants of Florence are proud custodians of their heritage, but also welcoming and open, ready to share the wonders of their city with those ready to discover them.

Florence is a city that invites you to explore, to dream, to discover. It's a place where every stone, every street, every smile tells you a story and offers you an experience. It's a city that awaits you, ready to gift you unforgettable days between the beauty of the past and the energy of the present. How can one resist the call of a city that has so much to offer, welcomes you with open arms, and invites you to become part of its ongoing story?

THE HISTORY MEDICI AND PAZZI FAMILIES

In my opinion, to understand Florence and to know it better, it's necessary to have a small idea of the history behind these walls and these fantastic monuments. Very often, you will hear about two very important families, the Medici and the Pazzi.

Florence was the cradle of the Renaissance and has roots tracing back to Roman times, but it was in the Middle Ages and the Renaissance that the city truly flourished.

The dawn of the **Medici dynasty**, a family of bankers, marked a significant turning point in Florence's history. Cosimo de' Medici, and later his grandson **Lorenzo the Magnificent**, were grand patrons of the arts and sciences, transforming Florence into an epicenter of culture and innovation.

Simultaneously, another noble family, **the Pazzi**, was active in Florence. The rivalry between the Medici and Pazzi culminated in 1478 with the **Pazzi Conspiracy**, a failed plot to assassinate Lorenzo and his brother Giuliano. This event accentuated the power of the Medici and their position as the primary patrons of the arts, attracting artists and thinkers like **Leonardo da Vinci and Michelangelo**.

Under the patronage of the Medici, Florence became a beacon of art, culture, and politics, with an impact that resonated across Europe. The city became a symbol of the Renaissance, an era of rebirth in the arts and sciences, and humanistic thought.

NAVIGATING FLORENCE

THE FLORENCE PASS

The first step to making the most out of your 2-day journey in Florence is securing the Florence Pass. This ticket unlocks the doors to the city's most illustrious monuments and museums, ensuring your time is spent soaking in art, **not standing in lines**.

Here's what the Florence Pass grants you:

- A rendezvous with Brunelleschi's Dome, where you'll stand under the shadow of architectural genius.
- A stroll through the corridors of the Uffizi Gallery, with an audio guide whispering the secrets of the masterpieces cradled here.
- The enchanting halls of the Accademia Gallery await, with an audio guide to accompany you through the whispers of the past.
- An audio tour of Florence boasting over 70 points of interest, perfect for peeling back the layers of this ancient city at your own pace.
- Plus, enjoy a 10% discount on a variety of other Florence activities, an invitation to delve deeper into the heart of Tuscany.

Alternatively, you can purchase individual tickets, but do it in advance so you'll skip the lines.

Ah, navigating through Florence, where every cobblestone pathway seems to tell a tale of the past. Given the city's compact and pedestrian-friendly nature, exploring on foot is indeed a delightful and common choice. You'd find yourself meandering through narrow ancient streets, discovering hidden piazzas, and suddenly standing before majestic Renaissance architecture.

On Foot:

The heart of Florence is best explored on foot. It's a relatively small city, and many of its treasures are located close to each other. You'd be able to soak in the city's ambiance at a leisurely pace.

Bicycles:

Renting a bike can also be a fabulous way to cover more ground and still be engaged with the city's charming ambiance. There are several bike rental shops and even guided bike tours available.

Public Transportation:

While the core of Florence is easily walkable, if you wish to venture a bit farther or rest those feet, the city has a network of buses. The buses cover routes within the city and surrounding areas. A single ticket is valid for 90 minutes, and 24-hour or multiple-day passes are available. You can download the app on the official website https://www.at-bus.it/en

Taxis and Ride-Shares:

Taxis and ride-sharing services like Uber are also available. However, do note that they can't always access the narrower or pedestrian-only streets in the center.

Car Rentals:

Having a car will be beneficial to explore the Tuscan countryside. Therefore, we will rent one later on in our journey, consider if you'd like to visit attractions far from the historical center you might do it the second day.

However, parking can be tricky, and there are many pedestrian zones (ZTL zones) in the city where driving is restricted.

Scooters:

Renting a scooter can be a fun and quintessentially Italian way to get around, although it's recommended for those familiar with riding scooters and the Italian driving style. (you will soon understand that we are not cautious drivers).

ACCOMMODATION

If you already know the dates of your journey (or as soon as you do!), it's crucial to book your accommodation.

Since Florence is one of the most tourist-frequented cities in the world, hotels that offer the best value for money often get booked up months in advance.

With only 2 days to explore the splendors of Florence, I highly recommend selecting accommodation nestled in the heart of the historic center. By doing so, you'll find yourself merely a stone's throw away from iconic cultural treasures such as the majestic Duomo of Santa Maria del Fiore, the illustrious Uffizi Gallery, and the charming Ponte Vecchio. Embracing the morning with a light stroll amidst the timeless streets, you'd effortlessly reach these landmarks, soaking in the essence of Renaissance with each step.

Now, among the cradle of history that is the center, certain neighborhoods stand out for their unique allure.

Santa Maria Novella area presents a blend of convenience and tradition. The ease of transit for those keen on exploring the broader Tuscan tapestry, coupled with proximity to central landmarks, makes it an appealing choice. Plus, the array of cafes, restaurants, and shops around means you're never far from a delightful Italian meal or a quaint souvenir.

Santa Croce is another captivating choice, where the rhythm of local life harmonizes with the historical resonance echoing through its streets. The namesake basilica, Basilica di Santa Croce, is a gem worth exploring, and the neighborhood's lively piazzas are perfect for enjoying a serene evening under the Tuscan sky.

San Frediano is a pretty and less trodden area, known for its artisan workshops and authentic Florentine ambiance. Here, the local eateries and small boutiques provide a slice of the city's true character, but a little funder out.

DAY 4

BASILICA DI SANTA MARIA NOVELLA

Our exploration of Florence begins with the Basilica of **Santa Maria Novella**, conveniently close to the train station. The interior of this Basilica is meticulously detailed, with frescoes on its walls depicting the daily life of medieval Florence.

Highlights include **La Trinità di Masaccio** (Masaccio's "Trinity") and **Il Crocifisso di Brunelleschi** (Brunelleschi's "Crucifix") which underscore the basilica's rich artistic legacy.

Il Chiostro Verde (The Green Cloister), adorned by Paolo Uccello, leads to the Spanish Chapel (Cappella Spagnola) with its important frescoes..

GALLERIA DELL'ACCADEMIA

Our next stop, only a few minutes away, is the famous **Galleria dell'Accademia**. On our way there we can stop for a good cappuccino at **Gocce's Bar Florence;** their chocolate-filled croissants or pistachio cream ones are one of those delicacies I miss so much since I've been living in the United States, so don't miss out on them!

As the morning sun shines, the excitement of exploring a piece of the Renaissance is in the air. Right in the middle of Florence, the gallery invites us with a peek into a rich past.

Stepping inside, we meet the giant statue of **David by Michelangelo,** standing tall and strong, a symbol of an upcoming battle with Goliath. The morning light highlights every detail of this 5-meter-tall (more than 16 feet) masterpiece. It's amazing to think that Michelangelo turned a huge block of marble into this iconic statue over three years back in 1500.

Walking through the gallery, we move from one room to another, each filled with beautiful art, music, and stories from a long time ago. The Galleria, started in 1784 for young artists to learn, now holds a rich collection of art, second in fame only to the Uffizi in Florence.

Moving from one artwork to another, the beautiful past of Florence comes alive. The gallery isn't just a place to see art; it's a page from Florence's grand story, blending the city's past and present.

Stepping back outside, the image of David stays with us as we move on to the next adventure in this historic city. The Galleria dell'Accademia is more than a tourist stop; it's a start to our exciting journey in Florence, with more wonders waiting to be discovered.

DUOMO – GIOTTO'S TOWER – BATTISTERO

Our Florentine escapade gracefully transitions as we make our way to the awe-inspiring **Piazza del Duomo**, just a brief 500-meter walk from the Galleria (just as a reference a meter is pretty similar to a yard). Here, we find ourselves standing at the feet of the iconic **Cathedral of Santa Maria del Fiore**, fondly known as the Duomo di Firenze. The cathedral, a labor of love and artistry, took nearly 140 years to complete, now standing as one of the grandest cathedrals worldwide, only shadowed by Saint Peter's in Rome and the Duomo in Milan.

As we approach, the cathedral's detailed Gothic architecture sweeps us off our feet. Its white and green marble exterior stands as a testament to the architectural prowess of the bygone era. However, the crowning glory of this majestic structure is undoubtedly **Brunelleschi's Dome**, stretching 45 meters (147.6 feet) in diameter and soaring 115 meters (377.3 feet) in height. The sight is nothing short of magnificent, and the intricate paintings adorning its interiors depicting scenes from the Last Judgment add a touch of awe-inspiring reverence to the experience. The dome of Brunelleschi remained white for more than 100 years until Cosimo de' Medici decided to hire Giorgio Vasari in 1572. Inspired by the Sistine Chapel, Vasari chose the theme of the Last Judgment. The work, initiated by

Vasari, was continued after his death by Federico Zuccari, who completed it in 1579.

The call to ascend to the top of Brunelleschi's dome is irresistible. Though a slightly demanding climb **of 463 steps** awaits, the promise of what lies ahead spurs us on. With each step, the anticipation builds, and as we finally step onto the top, it's a surreal moment. The panoramic vista of Florence from up here is nothing short of a visual feast, making every step of the ascent a worthy endeavor.

As we stand there, catching our breath, the sprawling city below seems to narrate stories of the Renaissance, blending seamlessly with the modern rhythm of life. It's a view that imprints itself in our hearts, etching a memory as enduring as the city's timeless beauty.

What to see in Piazza Duomo

Now that you find yourself standing in the majestic Piazza del Duomo, the heart of Florence, the journey through this ancient city during your two-day voyage unfolds further. The square is a treasure trove of architectural and historical gems, each holding tales of bygone eras.

As you gaze around, the towering **Giotto's Bell Tower**, or Il Campanile di Giotto, belonging to the Cathedral of Florence, beckons. If your legs are still sprightly after the climb to the dome, a venture up the **414 steps** of the bell tower awaits. Though the ascent might quicken your pulse, the sight from atop is a tad less clear compared to the dome, yet holds its own charm.

Adjacent to it, stands the **Baptistery of San Giovanni**, an octagonal marvel adorned in white and green Prato marble. This ancient place of worship, believed to have been a pagan temple dedicated to Mars in medieval times, is where many of Florence's eminent figures, like the illustrious poet, Dante Alighieri (the Divine Comedy), were baptized. Its alluring mosaic adornments and 3 **golden bronze doors** are a sight to behold. A modest attire is suggested to honor this sacred place, keeping in mind to cover legs and shoulders as you step in through the North Door on Via Martelli.

Your next stop could be the **Museo dell'Opera del Duomo**, a short walk away, housing sculptures and artworks once embellishing the cathedral. The museum also offers an unobstructed view of the dome from its beautiful terrace, enriching your understanding of the artistic legacy.

Just five minutes walking, for we will find the beautiful **Piazza Della Signoria!** No worries for today; we just going to relax at this point. We will be back at Piazza Della Signoria tomorrow so right now, enjoy the view and discuss the most important topic!

FOOD

I know we haven't yet discussed dining, even though lunchtime has long passed. But since all my favorite spots are clustered near **Piazza della Signoria,** I've decided to create a special section to guide you on where to grab lunch, enjoy an aperitif, and, of course, have dinner.

For **lunch**, I suggest grabbing a sandwich or a slice of pizza on the go to keep up with your adventure in this stunning city that has so much to see.
My preferred spots include **'All'antico Vinaio'**—be prepared for a wait, as the line is usually quite long, but they're quick to serve. And if you look them up on Google, you'll see they have over 35,000 reviews as we approach the end of 2023. Another fantastic option for a quick bite is **'Dal Vinaio,'** where the lines are shorter, but the sandwiches are just as famous.

For an aperitivo, a drink, or a snack, here 2 very nice alternatives a stone throw away:
Bar Uffizi: This bar is located right next to the Uffizi Gallery, and it is a popular spot for aperitivo. They offer a wide variety of drinks and snacks, and the prices are reasonable.

Antico Caffè del Moro: This cafe is located a short walk from the Uffizi Gallery, and it has been serving aperitivo since the 19th century. They offer a variety of classic Italian drinks and snacks, and the atmosphere is very charming.

Babae across the river. It's a charming place, especially known for its 'wine hole'(buchette) —a delightful historical tidbit as these small windows were used in medieval times to pass a glass of wine to passersby. Today, Babae has revived this tradition, and you can order a glass of wine or an aperitif and enjoy it on the street, served through a 'Buchetta' (thanks to the 'buchette' foundation for the photo).

When it comes to dinner, the choices are abundant. **'Trattoria dell'Oste'** boasts fabulous steaks, or for local dishes near Ponte Vecchio, at **'Trattoria Ponte Vecchio'** is where quality meets price. **Golden View Firenze restaurant** for an elegant atmosphere and Arno's river view.

FIRENZE FOOD

Beside, a QR code where I periodically save my favorite places. You can subscribe and receive updates on each new addiction. Click on the QR link, and by connecting with your Google Maps account, you can save the list.

DAY 5

PIAZZA DELLA SIGNORIA

Good morning and welcome to the second day. As usual, we'll start with a good coffee and cappuccino. Please refer to my online map for all the locations, depending on where you're staying. This morning we set out from **Piazza della Signoria**.

Piazza Signoria

This square is a treasure trove of historical and artistic landmarks. The centerpiece? The imposing **Palazzo Vecchio**, This fortified palace, with its robust, fortified tower, pierces the sky, a statement of political power from the time of the Florentine Republic.

The palace's facade is a tapestry of history, with its series of coats of arms telling stories of the city's ruling families. The front door, grand and welcoming, is flanked by a copy of Michelangelo's David on one side and Bandinelli's Hercules and Cacus on the other, standing as silent guardians of the city's culture and might.

Piazza Signoria David

Stepping inside, you enter a world of grand halls and intimate chambers, each whispering tales of political intrigue and artistic splendor. **The Salone dei Cinquecento** is vast, its ceilings lofty, adorned with magnificent frescoes and its walls lined with artworks that have witnessed the ebb and flow of Florence's fortunes.

The palazzo is not just a museum but a living part of the city, its offices still bustling with the day-to-day of civic life, as it has for centuries. Walking through its halls, you're treading the same stones as Medici dukes, Savonarola's reformers, and the myriad of artists and thinkers that shaped the Renaissance.

Moreover, for those **seeking more unique experiences**, there are special tours that include visits to areas usually closed to the public, such as the secret passages.

Additionally, while you're there, you absolutely have to check out the **Loggia dei Lanzi**. This open-air sculpture gallery is practically a playground for art enthusiasts, showcasing an abundant collection of classical masterpieces.

Completing the majestic tableau of Piazza della Signoria, the **Fountain of Neptune** stands as a symbol of the Medici family's grandeur and influence. Commissioned by Cosimo I de' Medici in 1559 to commemorate the marriage of Francesco de' Medici to Joanna of Austria, the fountain was conceived by Baccio Bandinelli but ultimately crafted by Bartolomeo Ammannati. Adorned with an array of mythological figures, it serves not only as a tribute to the union but also as a representation of Cosimo's dominance. The sculpture is particularly notable for its unique embellishments, such as the **Zodiac signs on Neptune's chariot**. The unusual portrayal of Virgo as a bride, complete with a unicorn, adds layers of biblical symbolism and alludes to the purity of Christ. Furthermore, the use of 'mischio' marble underscores the Medici's control over both the Mediterranean and the Tuscan terrain, weaving together art, mythology, and the power of nature in a single monumental work.

Fountain of Neptune

GALLERIA DEGLI UFFIZZI

Conveniently situated nearby is the world-renowned **Uffizi Gallery**. If you're an art aficionado, this is your sanctuary. The museum houses an astonishing array of works from the Renaissance era, including pieces by legends like **Michelangelo, Leonardo da Vinci, Raffaello, Caravaggio, Gotto, Botticelli, and the list goes on and on**. Whether you decide to explore this treasure trove independently or opt for a guided tour, your senses will be enchanted by the cultural richness encapsulated within the Uffizi's walls. Please purchase your ticket in advance.

PONTE VECCHIO

I know this day has flown, and we reach the gorgeous **Ponte Vecchio**. This medieval stone bridge is like no other, offering more than just a crossing over the Arno River.

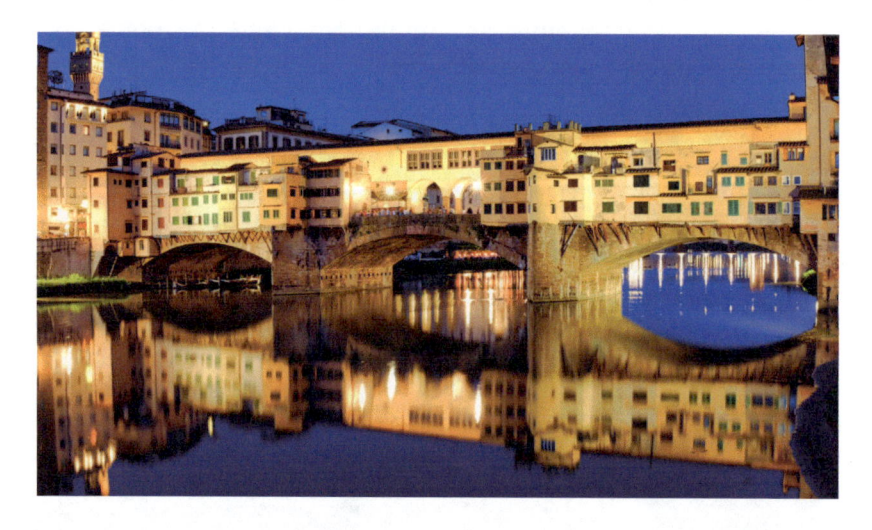

The Ponte Vecchio stands as the emblem of Florence, much like the Colosseum does for Rome. Built in 1345, it is one of the oldest stone bridges in Europe. Originally, in the 15th and 16th centuries, it was lined with butchers and slaughterhouses, but things changed when the Medici family moved to the Palazzo Pitti. Ferdinando I (the first) decided that the odors emanating from the bridge were unpleasant and thus shut down the butcheries, replacing them with jewelry shops and goldsmiths.

Florence is a treasure trove of wonders, and although time may be short, the **Boboli Gardens** are a must-see. These aren't just any gardens; they are a grand monumental park that warrants at least two to three hours for a thorough visit. As you wander among the ancient trees, you'll discover an extensive collection of sculptures, enchanting fountains, and quaint spots perfect for relaxation. Don't miss the terraced area where you'll find the Kaffeehaus, a rare example of Rococo architecture in Tuscany, and the Limonaia, home to various citrus species. The Boboli Gardens enchant in every season, providing a magical atmosphere that inspired many European royal gardens, including the famed Versailles. It's only when you are there that you can fully understand why. And to end your day beautifully, enjoy an aperitif at the **Loggia Roof Bar in the Hotel Palazzo Guadagni** for the perfect final touch.

Boboli Garden

DAY 6
TOSCANA

Let's start the day with the charming ritual of a morning coffee, perhaps a cappuccino, and a delightful pistachio croissant. After this small indulgence, we'll wander to the car rental agency I recommend:

Tuscany by Car Borgo Ognissanti, 142r, 50123 Florence conveniently located a short walk from the Santa Maria Novella station, and well-rated as one of the finest in Florence. Insurance, a necessary formality for car rental, is included in our basic package. Of course, if you wish to add extra coverage, feel free to do so.

With paperwork out of the way, we might jest about picking up a Ferrari or Lamborghini….. yet, opt for a more suitable ride, such as a Fiat 500. It's the smart choice for navigating the quaint, often narrow roads we'll encounter on our journey. Rest assured, the destinations we have in mind are well worth the drive.

A word to the wise: don't forget to request an automatic car. While manual transmissions are the norm in Italy, an automatic will make for effortless touring through the Tuscan landscapes, and I know this is what you all prefer!

Are we ready then? **The Chianti hills are calling**.

The journey through the Chianti hills is as enchanting as the destinations themselves. As you meander through this storied region of Tuscany, you are greeted by panoramic landscapes that are breathtaking. Vistas stretch over vineyard-clad slopes, and each bend in the road offers a new and spectacular view that seems painted with the very essence of Italy.

Given Tuscany's vast expanse and the abundance of sights to behold, I won't provide a precise itinerary for these two days, but rather a selection of possibilities that you can consider day by day. Much will depend on where you choose to stay. I definitely recommend a Bed & Breakfast or, even better, an **agriturismo**. Often at these agriturismos, you'll have the chance to sample local products, and some are even wineries that produce the very wine you'll be tasting. Therefore, I will simply point out the towns worth a visit and the excursions I find most intriguing. This time, however, it will be up to you to organize your day based on your accommodation.

CHIANTI - SIENA

Next on our journey are several charming towns that I personally adore, each offering a unique expression of the Chianti area. However, due to our time constraints and our planned overnight stay in Siena, you'll need to make a selection. While it's not possible to visit them all, I recommend stopping at two or three towns at most. **Among these, San Gimignano** stands out as a must-visit destination, renowned for its picturesque beauty and historical significance

As you set your sights on the Chianti region of Tuscany, a tapestry of history and viticulture unfolds before you. The first town is **Greve in Chianti**, where the medieval architecture whispers tales of ancient Etruscan and Roman times.
The main square, Piazza Matteotti, is adorned with a tribute to **Giovanni da Verrazzano, the explorer who unveiled the New York Bay to the world**.

Greve in Chianti

Wine enthusiasts find solace and delight in the Wine Museum, and every **September, the Expo del Chianti Classico** offers a chance to indulge in local wines and Tuscan culinary delights.

A short jaunt away, **Montefioralle** beckons with its timeless beauty, its cobblestone streets and stone houses a testament to its medieval stronghold past. The Chiesa di Santo Stefano houses beautiful frescoes and whispers legends of Amerigo Vespucci's birthplace.

Montefioralle

The culinary heritage of **Panzano in Chianti** is unmatched, thanks to Dario Cecchini's Antica Macelleria Cecchini, where the art of butchery becomes a spectacle, and Tuscany's rich flavors come to life with his **Florentine steaks** and recitals of Dante's verses. The medieval fortress and the Romanesque Church of Santa Maria are the cornerstones of this village.

Panzano in Chianti

Radda in Chianti The town's compact size makes it ideal for leisurely exploration. Take a walk to the central square, Piazza IV Novembre, which hosts the town hall and a grand fountain, serving as a social hub for both locals and tourists. The Church of San Niccolò, with its beautiful art and architecture, is another must-visit spot.

Redda in Chianti

Venture further, and **Castellina in Chianti** reveals its Etruscan roots and medieval military significance. The Rocca fortress stands guard over the village, and the Archaeological Museum delves into the ancient stories of the region.

Castellina in Chianti

SAN GIMIGNANO

It is known as the "Medieval Manhattan" for its distinctive towers that soar into the sky, and is a small gem nestled in the heart of Tuscany. Its historic center, a UNESCO World Heritage Site, envelops you with its ancient charm as you dive into the past.

The Towers: The towers are undoubtedly the symbol of San Gimignano. Once, there were about 72, erected by the noble families of the city as a symbol of power and wealth. Today, 14 remain, and the tallest is the **Torre Grossa**, standing at 54 meters. If you're not daunted by the idea of climbing a few steps, (after Firenze you should be ready) the view from the top is breathtaking!

Piazza della Cisterna and Piazza del Duomo: These squares are the beating heart of the city. Piazza della Cisterna, with its triangular shape and central well, is surrounded by well-preserved medieval buildings. Piazza del Duomo, on the other hand, is home to the Collegiate Church of Santa Maria Assunta, a Romanesque church with interiors that conceal true artistic treasures.

Collegiate **Church of Santa Maria Assunta**: This is a magnificent example of Romanesque and Gothic architecture. The interior, simple and austere, houses frescoes from the Florentine and Sienese school of the 14th century that vividly and colorfully depict biblical stories.

San Giminiano

Rocca di Montestaffoli: This ancient fort offers another marvelous panoramic view of the city and the surrounding Tuscan hills. It's an ideal place for a peaceful walk or to enjoy some rest in the shade of the trees.

Gelato: One cannot leave San Gimignano without trying a gelato from **Gelateria Dondoli**, located in Piazza della Cisterna. It is famous for its unique flavors and excellent quality, having been awarded the title of **world champion gelato maker**.

There are numerous charming small towns like Castelnuovo Berardenga, Castello di Brolio, and Colle Val d'Elsa that I could list, all of which I've indicated on the attached map for your convenience. You can download this map using the QR code provided.

SIENA

Siena is indeed one of Tuscany's most visited cities. While Florence and Pisa remain the most popular the awe-inspiring sights in Siena, like the vast Piazza del Campo or the stunning white marble facade of the Siena Cathedral, assure that there's much to see and you won't be disappointed.

Siena's charm lies in its well-preserved medieval streets and squares, rich history, and vibrant cultural scene. It's a city that effortlessly combines its historic past with a lively present, making it a must-visit destination for those exploring Tuscany.

Whether you're strolling through its ancient alleys, admiring its architectural wonders, or experiencing its unique traditions like the **Palio horse race**, Siena offers an unforgettable experience that beautifully complements the more frequented Tuscan cities.

Duomo di Siena

To reach the majestic Siena Cathedral, dedicated to Santa Maria Assunta, you need to walk along Via Fusari, which is filled with unique shops selling colorful ceramics. You'll immediately notice the style shared with the major religious buildings in Florence and Pisa, featuring imposing exteriors in white marble combined with darker tones that take your breath away.

Duomo Siena

The lower part of the facade was created by Giovanni Pisano, and the style is Romanesque-Gothic. The rear part of the cathedral, facing northeast, overlooks the Baptistery of San Giovanni. The bell tower, standing 77 meters tall, also follows the Romanesque style with bands of white and green marble.

The interior is even more captivating and worth visiting, with its stunning, slender arches, a floor decorated with extraordinary art, and the Piccolomini Library, which boasts beautiful frescoes by Pinturicchio and his pupils, including a young Raphael.

There are numerous other works, including sculptures by Nicola and Giovanni Pisano, Donatello, Michelangelo, and Bernini, as well as paintings like the famous "Maestà" by Duccio di Buoninsegna.

Piazza del Campo

From the Duomo, it's easy to reach the famous Piazza del Campo and its full splendor is even more mesmerizing from the narrow Costa Barbieri street.

The shell-shaped square, lined with shops and restaurants, boasts beauty and architectural integrity, making it one of the most unique squares I have ever seen. It's also the symbolic location of the Palio di Siena, held twice a year. Many people sit on the ground, and many youngsters are seated: a unique tradition!

Overlooking Piazza del Campo are the **Palazzo Pubblico** and the **Torre del Mangia** In the center is the Fonte Gaia, where there used to be a spring, now replaced by a rectangular basin designed by Jacopo della Quercia.

The **Palazzo Pubblico** of Siena, which you've probably seen in many postcards and souvenirs, is a symbol of Siena and one of the most refined and inventive examples of Gothic architecture. It was built from 1288 to 1342 and was the seat of the Government of the Nine. Today, it houses the Civic Museum and the Siena municipal administration. The visit typically starts from the "entrone" of the Podestà Courtyard, where horses participating in the Palio gather before entering the square. From here, you can access the Civic Museum, filled with art masterpieces, including a large Gothic Chapel and the panoramic Loggia, facing south, where the city's nine rulers admired Siena's possessions up to the horizon. The 88 meter tall Torre del Mangia, accessible from the same courtyard, offers a view of the square and all of Siena from above.

Another must-see in Siena in a day is the **Loggia della Mercanzia,** located behind Piazza del Campo and part of the Circolo degli Uniti palace. This Gothic-Renaissance building features a wide open loggia with three high arches adorned with statues and rich capitals. It was built to enhance the Mercanzia Palace, housing the Arte della Mercanzia of the Republic of Siena, and represents an almost completely intact depiction of historic Siena!

The Sanctuary of Saint Catherine, the patron saint of Italy and Europe, was born here. Her birthplace was transformed into a sanctuary in 1464. The house consists of several rooms with various testimonies to her life: the Oratory of the Crucifix (where the crucifix from which she received the stigmata is kept), the Kitchen Oratory (built from what tradition claims to be the Benincasa family's kitchen), and the Bedroom Oratory, frescoed by Alessandro Franchi. At the entrance, there's a beautiful portico known as the Portico dei Comuni, to which every Italian commune symbolically contributed a brick.

Fontebranda is a source of water and also a source of myths and beliefs: The largest and most famous fountain in the Tuscan city is Fontebranda, located on the edge of the ancient city. For example, an old legend says that those who drink its water become lighter. The Sienese are usually accused of this. Saint Catherine of Siena was also born in the Fontebranda district in 1347; hence, it's called "La Santa di Fontebranda." Her house is located near the fountain. Fontebranda's origins date back to the Middle Ages, and to commemorate its history, a strange sound fountain was installed that reproduces sounds, noises, and conversations from 1337 every half hour for five minutes. Don't miss it!

What is Palio di Siena

The Palio di Siena is an exhilarating and deeply traditional horse race that is much more than a mere sporting event; it's the heart and soul of Siena, pulsating with centuries of history and local pride. Held twice a year in the stunning Piazza del Campo, the race turns this central square into a vibrant amphitheater, buzzing with excitement and anticipation. Ten horses and riders, representing different city wards or "contrade," compete in this breakneck race, which is as quick as it is intense, usually lasting no more than 90 seconds. The origins of the Palio stretch back to the medieval period, making it one of the oldest horse races in the world. The event is steeped in rich rituals and pageantry, with each contrada donning its unique, vividly colored flag and emblem. The days leading up to the race are filled with festive celebrations, parades, and banquets, fostering a spirit of community and rivalry. Winning the Palio is a matter of immense pride and joy for a contrada, often sparking spontaneous and jubilant celebrations. For spectators, the Palio di Siena offers a captivating glimpse into the heart of Tuscan tradition, where history, culture, and competition entwine to create an unforgettable spectacle.

When

The Palio di Siena takes place twice a year, on two separate dates. The first race is held on **July 2nd**, known as the Palio di Provenzano, in honor of the Madonna of Provenzano. The second race occurs on August 16th and is called the Palio dell'Assunta, celebrating the Assumption of Mary. These dates are deeply rooted in Siena's traditions and are consistent each year, drawing large crowds of both locals and tourists eager to witness this unique and historic event.

AGRITURISMO

I list here some of the most prestigious and highly reviewed agriturismos in the area, refer to the QR code to see more, with their respective links to Google and their websites

Il Poggiarello Siena
Address: Str. di Fogliano 35, Siena, Siena, Italy, Zip Code: 53100
An ancient farmstead owned by the same family for over 200 years. It offers four rooms and apartments in a style reflective of

its history, with a seasonal swimming pool, and a breakfast option featuring local products.

IL LAVANDETO
Address: Str. Massetana Romana 76, Siena, Siena, Italy, Zip Code: 53100
A recently renovated agriturismo, named after its lavender fields. It includes modern furnishings in guest rooms, a garden with barbecue and gazebo, and proximity to Siena's historic cente

Villa il Castagno Wine Resort & Restaurant
Address: strada provinciale 102 (strada per vagliagli) 2, Siena, Siena, Italy, Zip Code: 53100
Focuses on Tuscan wines, offering suites named after Italian master painters. It provides cooking classes, a restaurant with local dishes, wine and cheese tastings, and afternoon drinks by the pool

La Selva Agriturismo
Address: Strada del Pian del Lago 19, Siena, Siena, Italy, Zip Code: 53100
Set on nearly 100 acres near the Pian del Lago region, it offers a large swimming pool, a two-level garden, a terrace, and various trekking routes. Accommodations range from apartments to double and triple rooms

Agriturismo Poggiacolle
Address: Strada di Montauto 58, San Gimignano, Siena, Italy, Zip Code: 53037
Just 2 kilometers from **San Gimignano**, offering panoramic views from the swimming pool. The property includes vineyards, olive groves, green pastures, and woods, with the chance to see local wildlife such as pheasants, hares, foxes, deer, and wild boars.

DINNER

La Locanda dei Tintori: located in Via Dei Pittori 13, 53100, Siena is a renowned dining destination, highly praised by visitors and locals alike. It has earned an exceptional 5 out of 5 rating on Tripadvisor. Known for its Tuscan, and Central-Italian cuisine, this restaurant offers an array of delicious meals for both **lunch and dinner**. The price range for a meal here is from $21 to $64, providing options for various budgets without compromising on the quality or ambiance of the dining experience.

Il Bargello Via di Citta' 55 Near Piazza Del Campo Il Bargello's atmosphere and culinary offerings make it a commendable choice for those looking to enjoy traditional Italian and Tuscan flavors in a cozy and inviting setting. Its proximity to Piazza Del Campo adds to its appeal, making it an accessible spot for visitors exploring the heart of Siena

Osteria degli Svitati: captures the essence of Siena in its quaint trattoria setting, complete with a whimsical cherub-with-a-corkscrew emblem adorning its windows. Nestled close to the abode of Saint Catherine, one of Italy's patron saints, the restaurant offers a serene dining experience with the gentle sound of church bells in the background. Specialties include Tuscan aglione, a flavorful garlicky tomato sauce served with pasta or gnocchi, and their remarkable anchovies with parsley, tarragon, and cooked potatoes. The traditional Tuscan desserts, like almond Ricciarelli, fruit and nut panforte, and biscotti, are the perfect end to a meal, especially when savored with a glass of sweet vin santo.

Pappardelle al ragu di Cinghiale

DAY 7
VAL D'ORCIA

Here we are, on day seven of your adventure. I'm sure you had a splendid night at one of the agriturismo in the Siena or San Gimignano area. Now, it's time to set off for one of the most enchanting places (in my opinion) – the Val d'Orcia. If you have an image of a quintessential Tuscan postcard in your mind, this is precisely what Val d'Orcia embodies – vast rolling hills adorned with endless rows of cypress trees and vineyards.

Perhaps you've seen Ridley Scott's "Gladiator," and if so, you'd be delighted to know that some of its scenes were shot right here in this area. Remember that beautiful moment when Maximus walks towards home to reunite with his son and wife? That's Val d'Orcia!

Now, let's talk about tradition. When you're here, you absolutely must try the Pecorino cheese from Pienza; it's the epitome of perfection. And, of course, the wine – an integral part of Tuscan heritage and Italian culture. Many Italians take great pride in it, and rightly so. So, get your cameras or smartphones ready for some unforgettable photos and videos as we head towards Val d'Orcia.

It's about an hour's drive from here, give or take, but just like yesterday, the spectacle is guaranteed.

Before we set foot in Val d'Orcia, there's something important I need to explain. As we've already seen in the Chianti region, the primary grape variety in this area is Sangiovese. Now, what makes **Sangiovese** fascinating is how it expresses itself differently based on how it's treated and the specific hills it originates from. This means we can have the same Sangiovese grape yielding different wines like **Chianti, Vino Nobile di Montepulciano, or Brunello di Montalcino**.

Our first stop in Val d'Orcia will be the charming town of **Montepulciano**, where, as you might have guessed, they produce Vino Nobile di Montepulciano (not to be confused with Montepulciano d'Abruzzo, which is another excellent wine but unrelated to our current adventure).

On the other hand, our last destination in Val d'Orcia will be **Montalcino**, a town famous for producing Brunello di Montalcino. Now, you might wonder why I'm delving into this discussion. Well, it's because I'll be drawing comparisons between these two towns, even though they bookend our journey today.

I have such a deep passion for this type of wine that I could talk about it for days on end. However, I'll kindly direct you to my website, italyunveiled.com, or my YouTube channel, where I'll have the opportunity to delve into the world of Sangiovese, its wines, and the rich Tuscan winemaking tradition in greater detail. There, you'll find a treasure trove of information and insights to quench your thirst for wine knowledge.

MONTEPULCIANO & MONTALCINO

Montepulciano, is a medieval town perched on a hill, you can wander through the streets lined with Renaissance architecture, stumbling upon family-run shops and eateries, and of course, the cellars that cradle some of Italy's finest red wines. The heart of the town, Piazza Grande, is a square that has been the focal point for local life for centuries, bordered by the imposing

Palazzo Comunale which resembles Florence's Palazzo Vecchio. The cathedral here, although its facade remains unfinished, is a treasure trove of art, including works by Taddeo di Bartolo and Sano di Pietro.

Montepulciano

Meanwhile, **Montalcino** presents a different charm. It's a tranquil hilltop retreat with a past woven through with battles and legends. The Abbey of Sant'Antimo, which heralded the town's beginning, stands as a testament to time, echoing Gregorian chants that hark back to an era of French monks. The Palazzo Pieri whispers stories of royal stays and wartime resilience, while the Bibbiano Castle stands as a proud relic of the 9th century. The Civic and Diocesan Museum showcases sacred artworks, and for a closer touch of the local winemaking tradition, the Ciacci Piccolomini d'Aragona vineyard welcomes visitors for intimate tastings.

Montalcino

SAN QUIRICO D'ORCIA

San Quirico d'Orcia is another gem nestled in the heart of Val d'Orcia. This charming medieval village boasts cobblestone streets that lead to authentic architectural treasures. One such treasure is the Collegiata di San Quirico, a majestic Romanesque church dating back to the 12th century, with a beautiful facade and a captivating interior that bears witness to its rich artistic and historical tradition.

The **"Horti Leonini" garden** is a masterpiece of Renaissance gardening from the 1500s, blending English and Italian styles seamlessly. With its elegant flower beds, statues, and centuries-old trees, this enchanting park is perfect for a leisurely stroll. Moreover, the countryside and green hills that envelop the village offer breathtaking views and opportunities for hiking, as well as visits to vineyards and wineries.

However, what sets San Quirico d'Orcia apart is its prime location along the famous Via Francigena, a historic pilgrimage route. This makes it an ideal place to immerse yourself in the culture and spirituality of ancient traditions, adding a unique layer to your Val d'Orcia experience.

If you're not planning to stay in an agriturismo and hence not dining there, consider the beautiful area of San Quirico d'Orcia for your **evening meal**. At the **Antica Trattoria Toscana Al Vecchio Forno,** you will discover culinary excellence that is second to none. The wine selection is exceptionally high-level, and you will be delighted with the exquisite creations of Chef Matteo. This place epitomizes Tuscan cuisine, where each dish is a journey through the authentic and refined flavors of the region.

CHAPEL OF MADONNA DI VITALETA

In the heart of Val d'Orcia lies the Chapel of Madonna di Vitaleta, an architectural masterpiece that captivates the soul. This building stands as one of the most remarkable and photographed landmarks in the region.
The chapel perches atop a panoramic hill, surrounded by rows of cypress trees and golden wheat fields, offering a spectacular view of the rolling hills that creates a magical and enchanting atmosphere. If you're fortunate, you might even spot beautiful deer during your stroll in this serene setting.
Returning to the chapel's history, it was constructed in the 17th century and continues to be a destination for pilgrims and visitors alike. The exterior boasts a pristine white facade with a picturesque bell gable. Inside, you'll find a statue of the Madonna with Child, revered by the faithful.

PIENZA

Pienza, often referred to as the "ideal city" of the Renaissance, was designed by the renowned architect Bernardo Rossellino on the commission of Pope Pius II. Its historic center, declared a UNESCO World Heritage Site, boasts cobblestone streets, Renaissance palaces, churches, and breathtaking panoramic views of the surrounding countryside. It's like an open-air museum.

Pienza streets

Palazzo Piccolomini and Palazzo Borgia stand out as some of Pienza's most beautiful and significant palaces, while the Cathedral of Pienza, dedicated to the Assumption, serves as an excellent example of Renaissance architecture. Pienza is also renowned for its exquisite pecorino cheese, crafted from the milk of local sheep, which you can savor and purchase in the village's artisanal shops.

But before you hop back into your car, take a brief detour to the Elysian Fields. These stunning hills are where the memorable final scene of "Gladiator" took place, adding a touch of cinematic magic to your Val d'Orcia experience.

AGRITURISMO

I list here some of the most prestigious and highly reviewed agriturismos in the area; refer to the QR code to see more, with their respective links to Google and their websites.

Poggio ai Gelsi
Address: Str. per Pienza, Montepulciano, Siena, Italy, Zip Code: 53045
Nestled amidst the rolling hills of Montepulciano, Poggio ai Gelsi stands as a serene haven, offering guests the quintessential Tuscan retreat steeped in the tranquility of nature.

Farm Lucignanello
Address: Localita' Lucignanello 29, Pienza, Siena, Italy, Zip Code: 53026
Situated in the quaint locality of Lucignanello, this farm promises an escape to the rustic charms of Pienza, where traditional Tuscan elegance blends seamlessly with the pastoral landscape

Farmhouse Poggio al Vento
Address: Strada di Ripa D' Orcia Loc. Poggio al vento, Castiglione d'Orcia, Siena, Italy, Zip Code: 53023
Perched in Castiglione d'Orcia, Farmhouse Poggio al Vento offers a picturesque sanctuary where the whispers of the wind complement the breathtaking views of the Val d'Orcia.

Antico Podere La Martinella
Address: Via del Colle, San Quirico d'Orcia, Siena, Italy, Zip Code: 53027
Located near San Quirico d'Orcia, this ancient farmstead invites guests to step back in time, immersing themselves in a landscape rich with history and Tuscan heritage

Podere Spagliarda - Val D'Orcia
Address: Strada provinciale N. 53 Km 1.4, San Quirico d'Orcia, Siena, Italy, Zip Code: 53027
Podere Spagliarda emerges as a gem in the heart of Val d'Orcia, providing a serene backdrop for a quintessentially Tuscan adventure amidst the undulating hills of San Quirico d'Orcia.

I hope you've enjoyed these two days in Tuscany, that you've tasted the fantastic local wines like Chianti, Brunello, and Vino Nobile, indulged in the stunning scenery of these hills, savored the Florentine steak, and fully embraced the Tuscan hospitality. But we've come to the end of this part of the adventure!
I know you would love to stay here for weeks on end, but in this itinerary, as promised, I'll be covering just a short visit. Don't worry, though; I'll be writing another one soon for a 10-day stay in Tuscany.
As for dinner, I recommend staying at your agriturismo. The ones I've suggested are all top-notch. Alternatively, you can follow the earlier suggestion and stop by Quirico d'Orcia at the ancient Tuscan trattoria, "Il Vecchio Forno." It's a delightful choice for a memorable meal.

Florentine steak

DAY 8 – 9 and 10

AMALFI COAST

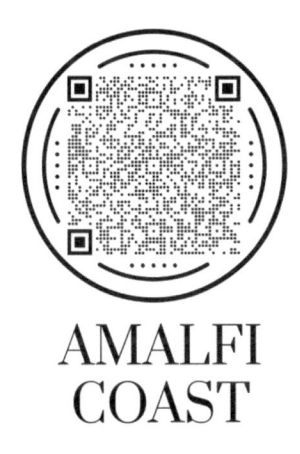

In the upcoming days, we'll be immersing ourselves in the breathtaking views and picturesque coastline of the Amalfi area. Given the diverse locations and the unique charm each place offers, it would be challenging to provide a step-by-step guide based on where you choose to stay. Instead, I'll take you through each town, providing comprehensive information about them, along with details on transportation options to seamlessly connect you from one enchanting location to another.

Transportation what to know

There are four main ways to reach the Amalfi Coast:
- By train, arriving at Naples Central Station or Salerno Station.
- By bus, with services to Sorrento, Salerno, or Naples.
- By car, offering the most autonomy and flexibility.

Traveling by Car: Driving is convenient but is far away. The route involves going to Rome direction, next to Napoli, exiting the A3 Napoli-Pompei-Sorrento highway at Castellammare di Stabia, and following the signs for Sorrento. This route offers fabulous views and the opportunity to travel along the coastal road, enjoying the scenic beauty. However, traffic can be an issue, particularly during peak seasons.

Traffic Considerations: Traffic in the Amalfi Coast area can be challenging, especially on certain days or periods like Ester, April 25th, May 1st (Italian national Holidays), during summer, and the Christmas season. Long queues are common along the SS 145 from Castellammare to Sorrento and the coastal road. It's advised to avoid traveling during these peak times to prevent getting stuck in traffic.

Parking Issues: Parking in the Amalfi Coast is limited, expensive, and extremely crowded during the high season. The average parking cost is around 8 euros per hour. To avoid parking hassles, it's recommended to choose a hotel with free private parking and use public transportation or rent a scooter or Vespa for local trave

Traveling by train

For detailed information on traveling by train in Italy, please refer to the "How to Get Around in Italy" section of this guide. It explains in detail the differences between the various types of trains and which ones are best for different occasions.

Reaching The Amalfi Coast Transportation

Wake up early, enjoy a delicious cappuccino and breakfast provided by your agriturismo, and get ready to hit the road. You have several hours of travel ahead of you to reach the stunning Amalfi Coast.

Now, depending on your preference, you have a couple of options to reach the Amalfi Coast.
First thing you have to decide in which town you like to spend the nights. I suggest booking in **Positano**, or the near **Sorrento**

as they usually have more availability and are a bit more affordable. Of course, if the price is not a concern, staying in Capri or Amalfi is truly a dream experience.

Regardless of the mode of transportation you choose to reach the Amalfi Coast, consider that it will **take approximately 5- 6 hours**, without traffic.
The 2 main points from which you can reach the Amalfi Coast, a small peninsula overlooking the Tyrrhenian Sea, are **Naples and Salerno**. Salerno is closer, but Naples has more options.

Firstly, check whether you **need to return the rental car to Florence** or if you're using a company that allows you to drop off the car anywhere. If you must return to Florence, the easiest way to reach the Amalfi Coast is by train.

Keep in mind that it's more than an **hour's drive to go back to Florence**, then a 3-hour train ride to Naples, or Salerno plus another hour on the bus or ferry (from Salerno)

Easiest and faster way

Traveling by train is by far the best solution.

Trenitalia (the Italian railroad Company) has services from Firenze central stations of Naples and Salerno, by high-speed train. So you can be on the Amalfi Coast in four hours and a half by train.

Alternatively, **if you can leave the car elsewhere (not in Florence)**, you can drive to Rome and take a train from there to either Salerno or Naples.

Flying isn't feasible as the nearest airport is in Naples, and there are no direct flights from Florence. You would have to fly via Rome, which is time-consuming and laborious. From Rome, it's much better to take a train, as it's faster and arrives in the city center.

To summarize, you either **need to get to Naples or Salerno** by train from Florence or Rome, from where you can take a ferry (a more scenic option than the bus) or drive for about five and a half hours to get there directly.

As I mentioned before, **the car must be left behind** because the roads on the Amalfi Coast are very narrow. Even the most experienced local drivers sometimes get stuck in traffic because someone cannot maneuver in the tight streets. Not to mention, parking is costly.

From Naples to Positano

- **Ferry**: Molo Beverello Port, Naples to Positano Ferry Terminal.
- **Bus**: Various stops in Naples, transfer in Sorrento, arrive in Positano.
- **Taxi/Private Transfer**: Direct from Napoli Centrale or Naples (it can be very expensive)

From Salerno to Positano

- **Ferry**: Salerno Port (Concordia Dock or Masuccio Salernitano Pier) to Positano Ferry Terminal.
- **Bus**: Varco 3 Bus Stop, Salerno, transfer at Amalfi, arrive in Positano.
- **Taxi/Private Transfer**: Direct from Salerno Train Station or Salerno.

Recommended Transportation Websites

Train Services

- Trenitalia: [Trenitalia Website](#)
- Italo Train: [Italo Website](#)

Bus Services (SITA)

- SITA Sud Transport: [SITA Sud Website](#)

Ferry Services

1. **Direct Ferries** - [Direct Ferries Website](#)
   - Offers a comprehensive comparison of different ferry services.
   - You can check schedules, routes, and book tickets for various ferry operators.
2. **Travelmar** - [Travelmar Website](#)
   - Specializes in ferry services along the Amalfi Coast.
   - Provides detailed information about routes, including from Salerno to Positano.
3. **Alilauro** - [Alilauro Website](#)
   - A well-known ferry operator in the region.
   - Offers services between various destinations, including Naples and the Amalfi Coast.
4. **NLG - Navigazione Libera del Golfo** - [NLG Website](#)
   - Operates ferries in the Gulf of Naples, including routes to Positano.

These resources offer up-to-date schedules, fare information, and online booking options, making your travel planning smoother and more efficient.

Welcome to the Amalfi Coast!

Welcome to the Amalfi Coast! You've arrived in one of the most enchanting places in Italy. To help you navigate through its picturesque towns, here are some practical tips

1. **Skip the Car**: The coastal road, SS 163, is scenic but challenging. It's narrow, twisty, and often crowded, especially with buses. Even locals find it tough! If you're here for the first time, driving can be more stressful than enjoyable.
2. **Public Transport**: For a hassle-free experience, opt for the SITA SUD bus service. With hourly buses, you can hop from town to town easily. Plus, it's a great way to mingle with locals and other travelers.
3. **Sail the Coast**: For a breathtaking view and a quicker journey, choose the Travelmar sea service. Glide along the coast, away from the traffic, and soak in the azure beauty of the Mediterranean.
4. **Scooter Adventure**: Feel adventurous? Rent a scooter for a day. It's a fun way to explore like a local, especially in the cool, serene summer evenings. Plus, you can venture between towns even when buses have called it a night.

Where to Stay on the Amalfi Coast

Remember, every corner of the Amalfi Coast has its own charm. Whether you're hopping on a bus, sailing the sea, or scooting around, you're in for a memorable journey!

You can comfortably base yourself in the same place and then move around from there to visit everything if you have more days. Praiano is the most central compared to Positano, Amalfi, Atrani, or Ravello.

The following are some ideas of hotel that you can find in the area there are hundreds of option for any kind of budget. Check my website www.italyunvailed.com for more information.

Le Fioriere Hotel is located in Praiano and offers a beautiful terrace.

Casa del Pescatore (Atrani): an economical solution in the historic center of Atrani with a charming view.

Luna Convento Hotel is in Amalfi and is located in an ancient 13th-century convent.

Villa Cimbrone in Ravello is a charming hotel that ranks among the most beautiful in Italy, surrounded by an English garden. Michelin-starred restaurant inside.

Just outside the center of Ravello is **Borgo Torello**, a less expensive but still very beautiful and bucolic choice.

If you're a little bit more on a budget, there are some option a little bit further out, You can look the towns like Agerola or Nocelle, or near Salerno, Cetara, Erchie, or Vietri sul Mare.

Costs

Although the Amalfi Coast is not famous for being an economical attraction, it's definitely worth the visit, and with some careful planning, you can save a bit.

Accommodation is the biggest expense, but Sorrento offers a wide range of options, from large hotels to small B&Bs, costing between 80 and 150 euros. Alternatively, you can book accommodation in lesser-known villages like Agerola or Maiori; however, consider transportation costs that might increase, ultimately leading to a budget similar to that of a higher-class hotel.

Another important aspect is that ferries are convenient but generally expensive as a means of transport, with prices ranging from 8€ to 20€ depending on the route.

For dining, depending on the category, a restaurant can cost on average from 30€ to 60€ per person (of course, not including the Michele stars restaurants). To avoid overspending on lunch, you can occasionally opt for sandwiches available in grocery stores or street food, with pizza being undoubtedly the favorite dish.

POSITANO

I know it's been a long journey to reach this heavenly place, but I promise the next two days will be absolutely fabulous. If you took the ferry, you would have already seen it for yourself. Admiring the beautiful scenery, regardless of your hotel's location, will be truly spectacular. Consider stopping for an aperitif to unwind, and then enjoy a leisurely stroll before dinner time. For dinner suggestions, please refer to the end of this chapter. And as usual, scan my QR code for some additional recommendations.

Famous places in Positano

Positano is a vertical waterfall of pink and yellow pastel houses that you can see going down and up small streets adorned with plants and flowers. **The Spiaggia Grande is the best place to see Positano** from above or from a boat.

The Spiaggia Grande is full of establishments with a small portion of free beach that is always crowded. However, it is also the location of the most famous restaurants and clubs.

If you want a **quieter beach, you can go to Fornillo beach** by climbing many steps.

However, the **real beauty of Positano** lies in getting lost in its uphill alleys, visiting the **Church of Santa Maria Assunta**, and stopping in a craft shop or a bar. It is imperative to take a trip to **Pasticceria La Zagara** to taste the best lemon sweets of the Coast.

Positano

For an aperitivo, you have the option of going to **Music on the Rocks**, which is practically the only nightclub on the Coast, or to **Franco's bar**, one of the most photographed bars of the **Hotel Le Sirenuse**.
In both cases, you will have a splendid view of the sea and Positano.

AMALFI

Amalfi, along with Positano, is the most famous and popular village on the Amalfi Coast, dating back to the powerful Maritime Republic era.

Piazza del Duomo, home to the magnificent **Duomo di San Andrea,** built in an **Arab-Sicilian style,** is the city center.

The colossal bronze door that was made in Constantinople and brought here by sea is spectacular, as is its polychrome facade. From the left side of the Duomo, you can access the Cloister of Paradise, built in the second half of the 1600s and housing the remains of important citizens of Amalfi. The historic center also has charming small alleys that you can walk through in a short time. You can stop by the historic **Pasticceria Pansa** to eat a lemon delight or the Santarosa: a ricotta and cream-filled sfogliatella, or both. For those who want to take a dip, there's the Spiaggia Grande, which has many establishments and a bit of free beach.

Amalfi

Amalfi, nestled at the mouth of a deep ravine, is not just about its famous Duomo and charming streets; it's a city steeped in history and culture. Once a maritime powerhouse, Amalfi played a significant role in trade across the Mediterranean, rivaling cities like Genoa and Venice.

The city's maritime legacy is celebrated in the Museo della Carta (Paper Museum), located in an old paper mill. Amalfi was renowned for its papermaking, and the museum offers a fascinating glimpse into this artisanal craft that played a vital role in the city's economy.

Walking through the town, you will notice the mix of architectural styles, a testament to Amalfi's varied historical influences. Besides the Arab-Sicilian elements, there are traces of Romanesque and Byzantine architecture, particularly in the smaller churches and ancient buildings dotted around the town.

For those interested in a unique culinary experience, Amalfi offers an array of seafood dishes, with fresh catches from the Tyrrhenian Sea. The city's restaurants and trattorias serve specialties like "scialatielli ai frutti di mare" (a local pasta dish with seafood) and "delizia al limone" (a lemon-flavored sponge cake), highlighting the region's lemons renowned for their size and flavor.

Nature lovers can explore the Valle delle Ferriere, a protected area behind Amalfi that offers **hiking trails through lemon groves and ancient ruins, leading to waterfalls** and rare plant species.

SORRENTO

Your exploration of Sorrento likely begins at the contemporary **Piazza Lauro**.

As you meander along Corso Italia, you'll reach the bustling **Piazza Tasso, adorned with statues of Sant'Antonino**, Sorrento's guardian, and the poet Torquato Tasso.
A detour up Enrico Caruso avenue leads to a captivating view of **Vallone dei Mulini,** a ravine underneath Piazza Tasso, home to remnants of a historical mill.
Piazza Tasso is ideal for savoring a coffee or limoncello, absorbing the lively atmosphere.
Venture further along **Corso Italia to discover the baroque Sorrento Cathedral** and the quaint Via Santa Maria della Pietà.

In the historic center, stroll through alleys lined with shops showcasing traditional wood carvings, lace, and limoncello.
The Tarsia Lignea Museum, showcasing exquisite wood inlay work, is a testament to Sorrento's rich craftsmanship.

Wander through the ancient Roman streets, visit the 14th-century **San Francesco Cloister**, and conclude your journey at Villa Comunale, boasting stunning views of the Sorrento Coast and Mount Vesuvius.
For a memorable meal, head to **Marina Grande**, where seafront restaurants offer exquisite local seafood.
After indulging in Sorrento's culinary delights, explore the historic center's shopping avenues, or relax on a sunny beach nearby or go to **I bagni della Regina Giovanna**

PRAIANO

Praiano is different from Positano and Amalfi as it is quieter and less crowded.
It doesn't have a real center, and the houses are scattered along the ridge of Monte St. Angelo, which sits 120 meters above sea level.

To reach the **beautiful beach of La Gavitella**, you need to climb many steps, about 300.

Then we can head south to **Marina di Praia, which has a charming small beach** and a marina from where boats depart for excursions. Today, in what were once fishermen's houses, there are several restaurants, including **Ristorante Da Armandino**, famous in the area for its high-quality dishes.

Continuing, you'll encounter the **Furore fjord**, which lies at the bottom of the fjord and hosts the tiny **Marina di Furore**, a small fishing village.

It's one of the most Instagrammed spots on the Coast.

Having an aperitivo on the **rooftop of Hotel Le Fioriere** is imperative if you arrive in Praiano at sunset. You can enjoy a spectacular sunset view over Positano and the sea from your vantage point. Making a reservation is essential.

Adding to this, Praiano is also known for its stunning views and serene atmosphere, making it a haven for artists and those seeking inspiration. The town's charming streets and pathways lead to hidden gems like small chapels and artisanal workshops. The **Church of San Gennaro**, with its beautiful majolica-tiled floor, is a must-visit for its mix of architectural styles and breathtaking sea views.

IL SENTIERO DEGLI DEI (FROM AGEROLA TO NOCELLE)

The Path of the Gods If you're sporty, you can't miss it! The Path of the Gods is considered one of the most beautiful trails in Italy and is thought to have been the only way to connect the villages of the Amalfi Coast for centuries.

In fact, the coastal road was only built by the Borboni (Bourbons) in the 1800s.

For years, the path was used as a mule track. Only recently has it been rediscovered and adapted to become a hiking trail. **The Path of the Gods starts in Bomerano**, a village of Agerola; there are buses that depart from Amalfi and stop in Bomerano.

You can walk to different paths the high path or the lower path. The scenic road of the high path starts in Bomerano and **ends at Santa Maria Del Castello**: Since it gains in elevation, it's a bit more challenging.

The lower path goes through Nocelle, and most tourists choose to do just that. The landscape is identical, with sheer cliffs overlooking the sea and enchanting views of the Amalfi Coast.

After reaching Nocelle, the center of Positano can be reached in about 500 meters on foot via a long staircase of 1500 steps. Alternatively, there is a bus service. Praiano is another option to reach the Path of the Gods; however, you will have to face a long staircase to get to the starting point. The trail is about 8 km long and takes an average of 3 to 4 hours to complete.

RAVELLO

Ravello, perched on the hills above Amalfi, is a true gem of the Amalfi Coast with its exceptional villas and gardens.

This sophisticated and elegant town, beloved by luminaries such as Richard Wagner, Virginia Woolf, and DH Lawrence, hosts the annual **Ravello Festival each summer**.

The exact dates can vary each year, but generally, the festival starts at the end of June or early July and continues until September or early October.

You can find more information and the specific dates for this year's festival on the official website: www.ravellofestival.info

This festival is a celebration of arts, featuring international concerts, ballets, exhibitions, and performances, drawing culture enthusiasts from around the world.

The journey through Ravello often begins at Piazza Duomo, leading to the entrance of **Villa Rufolo** and its 13th-century tower. Built in the 7th century by the wealthy Rufolo family, the villa has been home to numerous popes and Robert of Anjou, the ruler of Naples. However, Villa Rufolo is most renowned for **its stunning mid-19th-century gardens,** designed by Scottish botanist Scott Neville Reid.
These gardens boast lush flowers and offer breathtaking views of the sea and the coast, creating a picturesque setting that seems to blend art and nature seamlessly.

Not far from Piazza Duomo lies **Villa Cimbrone**, a villa dating back to the early 1900s, now an elegant boutique hotel with a Michelin-starred restaurant.
The English-style gardens here, with a terrace perched dramatically over the sea and lined with classical statues, are equally magnificent. **Villa Cimbrone holds a romantic allure**, having been a refuge for Greta Garbo and her lover. It has also welcomed distinguished guests like Winston Churchill and Salvador Dalí, adding to its rich tapestry of history.

But Ravello is more than just its famous villas and gardens.
The town's quiet streets, dotted with artisanal shops and cafes, offer a peaceful retreat from the bustling coastal towns below. Its elevated position provides a unique vantage point, offering panoramic views of the Mediterranean and the surrounding mountains, making it a haven for photographers and nature lovers. The combination of its artistic heritage, breathtaking scenery, and tranquil atmosphere makes Ravello my favorite destination in the Amalfi Coast.

CAPRI

Capri, often described as the pearl of the region, is an island of unparalleled charm and beauty.

Over a century ago, Charles Dickens wrote, "Nowhere in the world are there so many opportunities for delicious peace and quiet as on this small island."

This holds true even today. **Capri offers everything there is to see,** from the **Faraglioni to the Salto di Tiberio,** to the sparkling seas of Marina Piccola and Marina Grande.

It provides everything needed for a tranquil and relaxing life, devoted to enjoying the natural beauties under the warm Mediterranean sun, surrounded by the Mediterranean scrub.

To fully experience its splendor, spending several days is ideal but I know we have only one day.

But If you have a chance to spend more days and nights in the island I highly recommend splitting your nights between the bustling **Capri** and the more serene **Anacapri**.

If you're planning a day trip, start by taking the **ferry to Marina Grande**, then ascend to Capri town via the **funicular**.

Here, you'll be greeted with stunning panoramic views from the funicular's terrace and can witness the iconic Caprese clock tower in the bustling Piazzetta. (now you know where the name of the famous Caprese mozzarella and tomato dish is coming from!)

Stroll through **Camerelle**, the street famous for its chic boutiques, on your way to the breathtaking **Punta Tragara viewpoint**.

Don't miss the **Giardini di Augusto** (Gardens of Augustus), where you can marvel at the Faraglioni and the picturesque Marina Piccola.

Next, a taxi ride to Anacapri offers a change of pace.

Lunch at Sciuè Sciuè is a must, where you'll find delicious meals at reasonable prices. The chairlift to **Monte Solaro** is a

highlight, offering the highest and most spectacular views of the island. The descent back to Anacapri is equally mesmerizing.
For your return, take a **taxi directly to Marina Grande**. This route ensures you see every stunning aspect of Capri in a unique way.

Via Krupp in Capri

Of course, Capri isn't just seen from above; in fact, it's beautiful from the sea. So another option is to take a boat tour around the island to closely admire the **Faraglioni** and visit the various caves, including the Blue Grotto.

Blue Grotto, open from 9:00 AM to 2:00 PM, but only when sea conditions are favorable.

During the winter months, from November to March, it's quite rare for the grotto to be accessible. The cost to visit is around 20 euros per person, which includes the boat service with a rower and the entrance ticket. Accessible only at specific times, dependent on the tides, this stunning cave is entered in very small boats. The unique interplay of light and water inside the **Blue Grotto** offers an enchanting and unforgettable experience, highlighting it as a fabulous activity on any Capri adventure.

Blue Grotto

If you can spend a night here to truly soak in Capri's enchanting evening atmosphere and explore its hidden treasures.

The island transforms at night, offering a more intimate experience with its illuminated paths, quiet squares, and the soft sounds of the sea, making it an unforgettable part of any Amalfi Coast visit.

DINING

AMALFI COAST FOOD

When talking about dining experiences, or any other food and beverage options on the Amalfi Coast, please ensure to make a reservation before your visit (when is possible). Keep in mind that during the colder seasons, some restaurants may be closed. Therefore, if you plan to go during winter or late autumn, it's crucial to check whether they are open.

Many establishments on the Amalfi Coast have English-speaking staff, but if you encounter difficulties making a reservation by phone or on their website (as not all of them have one), Italy Unveiled offers a service to assist with reservations at restaurants where only Italian is spoken

Immersing yourself in the culinary scene of the Amalfi Coast is a sensory journey that never disappoints.

There are indeed many exceptional dining spots along the Amalfi Coast. My advice is to book a nice, upscale restaurant for a special experience. However, as you wander through the narrow streets of each town, you're likely to discover great restaurants offering more affordable prices. In this vibrant area, many menus are available in English. But if you stumble upon a hidden gem with a menu solely in Italian, that's the place I would personally choose to stop at for an authentic experience.

The following list is just to give you some references, but as I said, you will definitely find many other delicious places.

Sant'Agnello (near Sorrento):
Ristorante Calise, offers a seafood and Italian menu at mid-range prices.

Amalfi
Another gem is **Baglio Amalfi Italian Bistrò Cucina, Vino & Drinks**, perfect for savoring local cuisine in a welcoming atmosphere

Taverna Buonvicino, is another charming place to enjoy Italian, Mediterranean, and European dishes with a healthy twist

L'Abside in Amalfi is a must-visit for an experience that mixes seafood with Neapolitan tradition

Sorrento:
Porta Marina Seafood is an excellent choice, promising an authentic sea experience

Trattoria Da Maria offers traditional Neapolitan dishes in a family atmosphere

Ravello
Mimì Ristorante Pizzeria offering, in addition to a breathtaking view, Italian and Mediterranean cuisine and pizza appreciated

Enotavola - Wine bar - Palazzo della Marra is a picturesque place where wines are paired with local dishes.

For a snack or to taste the best limoncello, you must visit **Antichi Sapori d'Amalfi**, a shop located at the foot of the grand staircase leading to the cathedral of Amalfi. They not only offer traditional limoncello but also innovative varieties like juniper and peppermint-infused limoncello. Their specialty is the Sfusato lemons, with an intense and rich flavor, which makes their limoncello truly unique

These culinary experiences combine tradition with creativity, making every meal an unforgettable memory of your visit to these beautiful towns of the Amalfi Coast.

GOING BACK TO ROMA AIRPORT

Yes, we've come to the end of this fantastic 10-day journey through the heart of Italy, and now it's time to head back to catch the flight to the United States.

The best way is to take a **high-speed train** from either Naples or Salerno. In less than a couple of hours, you'll be in the center of Rome.

To the Fiumicino international airport

The non-stop Leonardo Express train to Rome Termini Station travels from Leonardo da Vinci Airport to Rome Termini in 32 minutes without intermediate stops.

It departs every 15 minutes during the pick hours otherwise it leaves every 30 minutes.

The first train from Rome Termini departs at 5:50 AM and the last at 10:50 PM from platforms 23 and 24.

On the Trenitalia website, a ticket for the Leonardo Express costs 14 euros each way and is guaranteed even in the event of a strike.

IN CASE OF EMERGENCY

When traveling in Italy, it's crucial to be prepared for emergencies, especially regarding health and safety:

- **24-Hour Pharmacies**: In every area, there's a pharmacy open around the clock ONLY ONE. Otherwise, the regular schedule is 9 AM, 8 PM in some places that might close for lunch.
The specific pharmacy changes daily; look for the schedule at any local pharmacy. These pharmacies offer essential medical consultations and medication services after regular hours. Otherwise, you can search on Yellow Pages online here the link. https://www.paginegialle.it/farmacie-turno
- **Medication and Prescriptions**: In Italy, certain medications that are prescription-only in the U.S. might be available over-the-counter, and some over-the-counter medications in the U.S. might require a prescription. It's advisable to carry your prescription or current medication with you for reference.
- **Accessible Healthcare**: The Italian healthcare system is known for being either free or requiring a small copayment. Emergency room (Pronto Soccorso) services are available free of charge, ensuring that both locals and travelers have access to necessary medical care.
- **Emergency Contact Numbers**: For police assistance, dial 113 or 112 and for medical emergencies requiring an ambulance, dial 118 (the ambulances for free as well). These numbers connect you to the respective emergency services promptly. Unfortunately, no many people had the

phone they will be able to speak in English, but I'm sure that they will try their best to help you.
- **Local Hospitals and Clinics**: Knowing the locations of nearby hospitals and clinics is beneficial. Major cities have well-equipped hospitals with emergency services (Pronto Soccorso), and clinics (guardia medica) provide care for non-urgent medical issues.
- **Language Considerations**: In tourist areas and major cities, hospital and emergency staff generally speak English, facilitating communication during emergencies, which might become a challenge in the country or small towns.
- **Consular Assistance for U.S. Travelers**: The U.S. Embassy in Rome and consulates in other cities offer assistance in emergencies, like lost passports or legal issues. Keep digital or photocopy backups of important documents for quick access in emergencies.

Remember, in any emergency, staying calm and clearly communicating your needs and location is crucial. Italy is well-equipped to handle a wide range of emergencies, ensuring a safe environment for travelers.

A HEARTFELT THANK YOU AND A SPECIAL GIFT JUST FOR YOU

Well, we've come to the end of an amazing journey! We have now reached the end of this fantastic 10-day journey through Central Italy, exploring the beautiful areas of Rome, Florence, Tuscany with the stunning Val d'Orcia region. We've learned to appreciate wines like Chianti and Brunello, savored local delicacies from Rome, Florence, and the Amalfi Coast, and

traveled from cities to mountains, hills, and the beautiful Amalfi Coast with its fabulous, crystal-clear blue sea.
All that's left is to bid you farewell and hope to meet you again on another 10-day adventure through Italy
I hope you've found this guide as delightful to read as it was for me to put together.

WEBSITE

Now, as much as we've seen, Italy has so much more to offer!

If you've loved this journey, you'll be thrilled to know that I have other guides detailing 10-day itineraries that explore other spellbinding regions of Italy. They're just a click away on my website, ready to inspire your next Italian getaway.

But wait, there's more! As a special thank-you for your support, submit proof of your purchase of this guide on my website, and I'll send you an exclusive link to a map featuring **over a hundred of my all-time favorite destinations across Italy**. Imagine it as your ultimate cheat sheet for experiencing Italy like a local!

Your encouragement keeps me going, scouting out Italy's most charming corners, and sharing them with you. From the bottom of my heart, grazie mille for being a part of this grand Italian experience.

Don't forget to catch all my latest travel tips and hidden Italian gems on my **YouTube channel @italyunveiled**

Here's to many more Italian adventures together!

Ciao for now!

Isabella Di Marco

Made in United States
Troutdale, OR
03/27/2025